A–Z

of

HEIRLOOM
SEWING

SEARCH PRESS

Contents

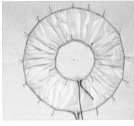

3   Introduction

5   Equipment
    Sewing machine
    Presser feet
    Needles
    Tools
    Pins
    Scissors
    Pressing tools
    Marking tools
    Measuring tools
    General tools

10 Fabric
    Interfacing

14 Machine sewing thread

14 Notions

16 Trims
    Lace

18 General instructions
    Preparation
    Preparing fabrics
    Preparing trims
    Cutting out
    Marking the fabric
    Templates
    Seams
    Starting and finishing

21 Pressing

21 Your finished project
    Laundering
    Ironing
    Storage

25 Entredeux techniques
    27 *Attaching entredeux*
        to entredeux
    28 *Attaching entredeux to fabric*
    36 *Attaching entredeux to lace*

39 Fabric techniques
    40 *Roll and whip*
    45 *Corded edge*
    47 *Madeira appliqué*
    53 *Puffing*
    59 *Tucks*

70 Lace techniques
    70 *Attaching lace to fabric*
    79 *Joining lace*
    80 *Neatening lace*
    81 *Attaching lace to lace*
    84 *Inserting lace*

91 Handworked edges and finishes
    91 *Baby ricrac edges*
    93 *Blanket stitch and buttonhole*
        stitch edges
    99 *Bullion scallop edge*
    100 *Crochet scallop edging*
    102 *Decorative thread*
        replacement
    103 *Faggoting*
    104 *Hem stitch*
    108 *Palestrina knot edge*
    109 *Ruched edges*

113 Construction techniques
    113 *Buttons and buttonholes*
    118 *Hems*
    124 *Piping*
    127 *Plackets*
    134 *Rouleau*
    136 *Seams*

Introduction

The term heirloom sewing is for most of us associated with fine delicate garments that have the look and feel of eras past. This fascinating style of sewing can be used to replicate traditional heirloom garments from a previous century, or may be used in innovative ways to create future heirlooms.

The combination of fabric, embroidered insertion, lace, entredeux, puffing and tucked panels result in creations of which dreams are made.

French hand sewing, as heirloom sewing was once known, was worked entirely by hand with many long and loving hours invested to produce baby garments and christening gowns, dresses, blouses, undergarments and household linens with which to fill a trousseau. With attention to detail you can duplicate these methods with your sewing machine and revisit more genteel times.

Miraculously, garments made with lace as fine as cobwebs have survived for centuries, providing us with the opportunity to study and marvel over fine garments worn at the French courts and later made in the Victorian era, when heirloom sewing was very fashionable. Heirloom sewing using fine laces, delicate fabrics and couture techniques has maintained a popularity with many twentieth century designers. Within the Metropolitan Museum of Art in New York, we can be amazed by a 1939 evening gown by Madeleine Vionnet or a 1995 design by Karl Lagerfeld.

Included in the A–Z of Heirloom Sewing are step-by-step instructions for these intriguing techniques, both by machine and by hand. Heirloom sewing by hand or machine can be enjoyable and very rewarding and as you turn the pages I hope you will be inspired and develop a love of fine and gentle sewing, creating your own heirlooms.

Lyn Weeks

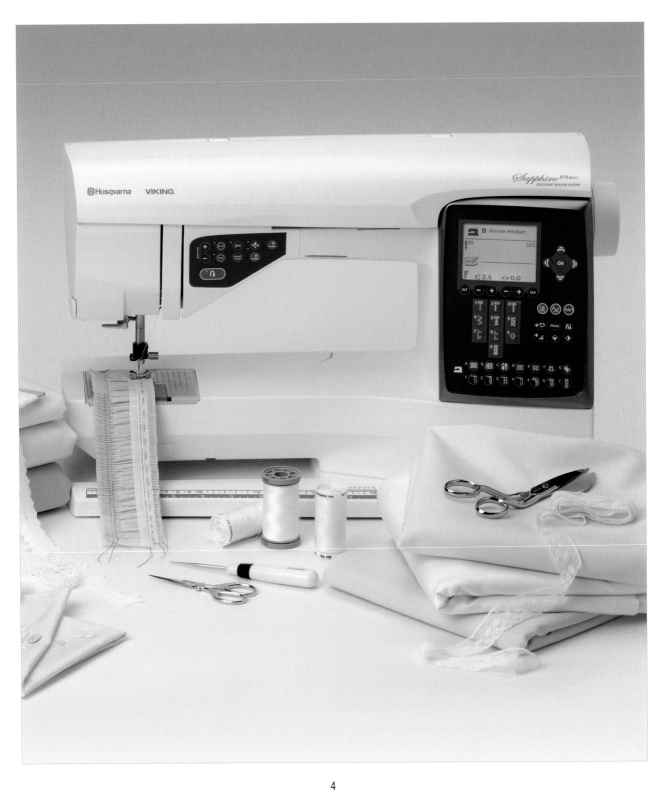

Equipment

Sewing machine

Today's sewing machines make it possible to imitate French hand sewing when creating heirlooms for the future. The mechanics of sewing machines are constantly changing with new technology, but the main principles have remained the same.

There are several things to consider when purchasing a sewing machine. It is advisable to ask for a detailed demon-stration that reflects the type of sewing, fabric and thread you will be using. Pay special attention to the top and bobbin tensions. An adjustable needle position is also very useful. Explore the selection of presser feet available to make sewing tasks easier. Ensure the machine has a suitable stitch selection and a good range of stitch lengths and widths. All sewing machines have different width and length settings that need to be slightly adjusted for different laces or entredeux.

Just as it is important to understand the balance between fabric, needle size and thread weight, you also need to know your machine well and ensure that it is set correctly for the task at hand. Study the instruction manual and attend any workshops that may be available.

Machine maintenance

Clean and oil your machine on a regular basis. Mechanical machines should be oiled according to the manufacturer's instructions. Electronic and computer sewing machines should be oiled as directed in the manual and serviced regularly by a professional.

The stitch settings recommended throughout are given as an indication only.

Presser feet

Every sewing machine comes with a variety of basic or the most commonly used presser feet, with additional feet available for more specific purposes.

The presser feet will vary slightly from one brand of sewing machine to another and will, in many cases, have a different name. The purpose of selecting a presser foot is to make the task easier and to achieve the best possible result. It is important to know the specific feet that are available for your machine. Experiment to determine the best and most appropriate foot for the task.

All-purpose foot

Also basic, standard or universal
This is the standard foot for all basic sewing. The foot has a smooth flat sole, providing control as the fabric passes over the feed dogs. It has an opening wide enough for a 6mm (¼") wide zigzag stitch, allowing clear visibility at the needle. It has an engraved centre line and an engraved line or opening on either or both sides of the centre line.

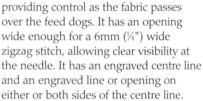

This foot is most suitable for sewing fine fabrics because it will put weight on the fabric while holding it firm in front of and behind the needle. Uses include all construction, especially French seams.

Manual

Buttonhole foot
Two grooves under the sole of the foot allow the fabric to move freely as the stitches build up to form the buttonhole.

In heirloom sewing this foot is also perfect for maintaining an even finish when working techniques involving rolling and whipping, with the 'rolled' edge being channelled in the left hand groove.

It is also useful for making and attaching fine corded piping, using a groove under the foot to guide the piping.

Jeans foot

Designed for sewing heavy seams and thick fabrics without skipping stitches or breaking needles, this foot is wider than either a straight stitch or ¼-inch foot, providing greater pressure and stability on the fabric and feed dogs. As the foot only has a small needle hole, it is important to always test the zigzag width to ensure it can be accommodated within the hole. A width of almost 1.5mm (⅝") can be achieved with a fine needle.

For heirloom sewing it is very useful for rolled and whipped hems and joining laces. The zigzagged roll will channel through the narrow groove behind the needle.

Edge-joining foot

The edge-joining foot has a metal guide along the centre. The most accurate of these feet will have a fine, permanent guide as opposed to a thicker adjustable plastic guide. The fine blade allows greater manoeuvrability when stitching curved edges and provides better contact when using lightweight heirloom fabrics.

While the edge-joining foot is most often associated with topstitching or straight stitching, it is also very useful for working with entredeux for both straight and zigzag stitching, where the blade is positioned in the ditch against the embroidered holes. Other uses include French seam, flat-fell seam, attaching entredeux to fabric and the various single needle pin tucks.

Open-toe or embroidery foot

This foot has been specifically designed for satin stitching and other compact stitches. The wide indentation on the sole of the foot that will accommodate a width of up to 6mm (¼"), allowing thick bulky stitches to pass under the foot without building up and inhibiting the flow of the fabric. The open area between the toes of this foot provides a clear view of the needle and the stitching area. It is also useful for appliqué techniques, hemstitching and other decorative stitches with a forwards and backwards stitch motion.

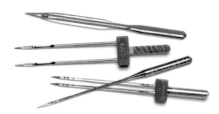

Twin needle foot

Most sewing machines have more than one twin needle foot, each with three, five, seven or nine grooves under the sole of the foot. It is used with a twin needle to stitch pintucks, spacing the tucks by positioning the previous tuck in one of the grooves.

The twin needle foot also provides stability when making mini piping with lightweight fabric. The piping or the needle is decentred to allow the stitching to be positioned close to the piping.

¼-inch foot, also patchwork or quilting

The ¼-inch foot has a narrow channel in front and a small indentation in the sole behind the needle. On some sewing machines there is also a metal bar on the right hand side of the foot. The bar is positioned against the edge of the fabric to accurately stitch a ¼" (6mm) seam.

A ¼-inch foot with markings on each side equal to the needle position and ¼" in front of and behind the needle simplifies the job of turning a corner when topstitching or inserting piping into a corner.

Pintuck

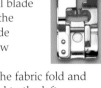

The foot has a metal blade along the centre at the front to act as a guide when making narrow tucks. The blade is positioned against the fabric fold and the needle decentred to the left, determining the width of the tuck.

Sewing machine needles

Sewing machine needles are available in different sizes, ranging from the finest, size 60 to the thickest, size 120. Choose a needle which best suits the type and weight of fabric you are using.

Replace the needle after approximately 8–12 hours of sewing time and discard any bent or burred needles, as they can cause irreparable damage to the fabric and trims. A damaged needle can also result in skipped stitches.

Needle	Description	Use	Size	Suitable for
Universal	Standard	Construction	60–70	Fine fabrics such as batiste, voile lawn and silk
			70–80	Medium weight cotton, fine linen winter weight fabrics
			80–90	Ticking, heavy weight linen
Twin needle	Standard needle with double shaft	Tucks, embroidery	1.6/70–2.0/75	Fine fabrics such as batiste, voile lawn and silk
			2.0/80–2.5/80	Medium weight cotton, fine linen soft winter fabrics
Jeans needle	Extra sharp thick shaft	Pin stitching, hem stitching	70	Fine fabrics where only a small pin stitching hole is desired
			110	All fabrics and lace, will not damage the fibres
Wing needle	Sharp with flat flange on each side of the shaft	Pin stitching		Fabric only as it will sever lace fibres

Tools

Basic tools such as a good pair of scissors, a selection of pins and needles, tape measure and marking pens are essential. Extending the basics and adding more specialised equipment can be done over time.

Pins

A wide variety of pins are available in all shapes and sizes. Using the finest, extra-sharp glass headed pins for heirloom sewing is recommended.

It is well worth investing in several packets of fine pins that will last for many years. Discard any pins that are bent, burred or damaged in any way. Store your pins in a sealed, moisture-proof container to prevent rust.

Scissors

Scissors are available with metal, plastic or 'soft-grip' handles. Choose a style that is comfortable to hold.

Ensure the blades are sharp right to the tips and avoid using your scissors for any other purposes than cutting fabric and thread. Have scissors sharpened as soon as they show signs of wear. Dead spots are a common sign. Take care not to drop scissors as this can damage them beyond repair.

Dressmaking scissors, have blades usually 18–20cm (7–8") long, making cutting easy. Use the full blade in a gentle squeezing motion when cutting, as this ensures a straight cut edge.

Small dressmaking or trimming scissors have finer, shorter blades, usually 12.5–15cm (5"–6") long. The blades are serrated allowing for accurate grading and trimming of fine, delicate fabrics.

Embroidery scissors are usually 7.5–10cm (3–4") long and have a fine blade, tapered evenly to a sharp point. Consider the fit when selecting embroidery scissors, as some are available with larger finger holes. A serrated blade is also a good option when used for trimming very fine fabrics as well as threads.

Duck-bill scissors have one sharp narrow blade and one wider blade with a rounded nib. They are ideal for trimming along seams and edges next to lace and entredeux and will help eliminate the risk of cutting the heirloom piece.

Hint

Avoid pinning across a seam allowance as it is possible to inadvertently cut into a pin, causing damage to one or both blades of the scissors.

Description	Head	Diameter	Length	Metal	Use
Couture	Metal	0.58mm	25mm	Stainless steel	Light and medium fabric
Dressmakering	Metal	0.50mm	30mm	Hardened steel	Delicate fabric
Dressmakering	Metal	0.60mm	30mm	Hardened steel	Light and medium fabric
Dressmakering	Metal	0.65mm	25mm	Hardened steel	Light and medium fabric
Glass headed	Glass	0.60mm	30mm	Nickel plated steel	Delicate and lightweight fabric
Glass headed	Glass	0.50mm	35mm	Nickel plated steel	Light and medium fabric
Lace	Metal	0.5–0.7mm	25–30mm	Stainless or nickel plated steel	Lace

Pressing tools

Iron

Irons can vary from simple models that cost a few dollars, to deluxe ironing systems that include large water reservoirs and suction boards. Common problems with irons are scale build-up in the water tank and a dirty soleplate. Using distilled water or buying an iron with a filter can help to alleviate the scale problem. Cleaning the iron regularly will keep the soleplate in good order. For pressing heirloom weight fabrics, lace and entredeux, select an iron with a 'shot of steam' feature.

Puff iron

This is an ingenious device for pressing puffed sleeves. The egg shaped tool is clamped to a table top and the sleeve is rubbed over the heated puff iron to remove any creases.

It becomes very hot so move the fabric quickly across the metal to avoid scorching the fabric.

Ironing board

Choose a sturdy board with a smooth padded cover. Keep the cover clean to prevent marks transferring to the fabric that is being pressed. An underpad of cotton batting is recommended, as it will absorb the heat, whereas a foam or other synthetic pad will reflect heat and can cause scorching.

Sleeve board

A sleeve board is a smaller version of an ironing board. It enables you to press a variety of garments and their components, such as sleeves in the round.

Pressing ham and roll

A pressing ham takes its name from its similarity in shape to the cured meat. It is a pillow of fabric, usually wool on one side and cotton on the other, firmly filled with sawdust, wool or cotton rovings. A ham is used for pressing small areas that are difficult to reach on a flat surface. It is also used for pressing curves and rolling collars.

A sleeve roll is similar to a pressing ham, cylindrical in shape. It is particularly useful for pressing sleeves and other parts of a garment that cannot be laid flat.

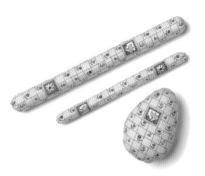

Pressing mitt

A glove shaped pressing device, the mitt is worn on the hand and pushed into areas that cannot be laid flat.

Pressing cloths

Chemically treated pressing cloths are known as Rajah® cloths. They are used when steam ironing and are excellent for setting pleats and removing creases. Rectangles of fabric such as organdie or organza are useful as pressing cloths for delicate fabrics, fusing interfacing and appliqué.

Flannelette or fine towelling is helpful when pressing embroidery. Fold the fabric into a pad, place beneath the embroidery and press from the wrong side of the embroidery.

Spray starch

Commercial spray starch can be purchased in aerosol and trigger-pump containers. Whichever you choose, the nozzle will need to be checked and cleaned regularly to avoid liquid spray starch being dispensed in 'blobs' rather than as a fine mist.

Misting with water is recommended for all preparation of lace, embroidered trims and fabric. Misting with spray starch and pressing once or twice after all joins are complete, provides stability during the construction process.

Marking tools

Always test the suitability of your marker on a scrap piece of fabric before you begin.

Chalk based pencils are excellent for use on dark fabrics. The chalk 'lead' is enclosed in a wood casing, making the pencil easy to use. The marks just brush away. Other forms of chalk markers are seam markers and tailor's chalk blocks.

Fabric marking pens are handy for transferring any temporary pattern or design markings onto fabric. There are several different types available so choose one that best suits your needs.

Water-soluble markers are chemical based and leave blue marks that can be removed with water. Always remove the marks before pressing, as heat will make the marks permanent. Water-soluble markers are best suited where the lines will be cut away as rinsing small sections will leave water marks.

Fading markers are also chemical based and leave a purple mark. The marks will fade away quite quickly depending on the fabric and the pressure used. Do not press before they fade.

Measuring tools

Dressmaking squares can be used for checking the straight grain of the fabric and determining the true bias. They are invaluable for ruling lines at right angles to each other.

Hem marker is a useful tool to measure the height of a hem above the ground, making it consistent around a skirt.

Measuring gauge This has a sliding tab that makes it easy to measure and repeat pleats and tucks. It is also used to measure the depth of a hem, the length of a buttonhole and the spaces between them accurately.

Tape measure is a pliable measuring device. Choose a tape that begins the numbering from both ends and is marked in imperial and metric measurements.

Wooden or metal rules are useful for marking long lines such as cutting lines, frills, bindings and bias strips.

Clear grid rule is available in imperial measurements only. It is 2" × 12" or 18" wide and made from thin, flexible Perspex. This rule makes it easy to measure and mark tucks, or square up cutting and/or stitching lines to the fabric edge.

Scallop radial rule is a clear Perspex grid rule with curves of varying widths, used for drawing scallops.

General tools

Lace shaping or blocking board is a homemade tool used when shaping lace. Use a large piece of foam core or the card centre from a bolt of fabric. Cover it with cotton wadding and calico that has been laundered well to remove any sizing and secure it tightly around the blocking board.

Memory curve or flexible French curve is a bendable rod that can be adjusted to any curved shape, ideal for shaping scallops.

Finger shields are usually made commercialy from rigid plastic, shaped to fit over the forefinger. You cam make your own from heavy plastic cut 2.5cm × 10cm wide (1" × 4"), wrapped around the finger and secured with electrical tape. A finger shield is essential for hemstitching by hand and useful for many other hand heirloom sewing techniques.

Loop turners are fine metal rods with a latch on the end, used to turn rouleau strips to the right side.

Needle threaders are small tools, very useful for threading machine and hand sewing needles. A hook style needle threader is recommended for reverse-threaded release tucks on page 64.

Thimbles are available in different materials such as plastic, leather and metal. A thimble protects the top of the finger that is used to push the needle through the fabric. Choose a thimble that fits snugly over your finger.

Fabric

When making beautiful garments it is recommended that you choose your fabric and other requirements carefully and purchase the best quality you can afford.

Batiste. A sheer, fine woven fabric with a plain weave of cotton, cotton blends, wool, silk, rayon or other fibres.

Broadcloth. A fine closely woven fabric, with very fine crosswise ribs, made from cotton or a cotton/polyester blend. Filling yarns in this plain weave are heavier and have less twist than the lengthwise warp yarns. The best grades are made with combed ply yarns of Pima cotton.

Cambric. A soft white, closely woven cotton fabric, calendared (treated by rollers) to give lustre on the right side. Originally made from linen in Cambrai, France.

Challis. One of the softest fabrics made, usually with a plain weave, originally made of wool, but now of cotton, rayon and a wide variety of blends.

Chambray. A soft fabric made with a plain weave, coloured warp and white weft yarns. The flat smooth fabric may be all cotton or a cotton/polyester blend. Chambray gets its name from Cambrai, France, where it was first made.

Combed cotton. The finest quality batiste is made with very thin yarns of combed cotton. All cotton fibres are carded, but only the finest cotton is combed. The combing process removes shorter fibres and impurities from the longer, more desirable fibres. Combed yarns are finer, cleaner, more compact and even than carded yarns. Fabrics made from combed yarns are tightly woven and more expensive than ordinary cotton fabrics.

Crepe. A general classification for fabrics with crinkled or grainy textures, woven with tightly twisted crepe yarns. These fabrics can be sheer or heavy, with imitations produced by treating with a chemical solution. The crepe-like effect is not always permanent.

Dimity. From the Greek word meaning 'double thread', Dimity is a lightweight woven cotton fabric similar to lawn. It is made by weaving two or more yarns as one and separating them by areas of plain weave, giving a checked or barred effect.

Dotted Swiss. A lightweight cotton or cotton blend fabric, woven from fine yarns embellished with woven or flocked small dots.

Flannel. Downy soft warm fabric that is brushed on one or both sides to raise the nap. Flannel is usually cotton or a cotton blend and can be woven with a twill or plain weave.

Georgette. Very fine fabric similar to crepe, made from very fine yarns.

Handkerchief linen. A lightweight fabric with a plain weave made from the flax plant. Handkerchief linen is similar in lustre to batiste but the yarns are more uneven than cotton yarns, often creating the 'slubs' inherent in this fabric.

Lawn. A lightweight cotton fabric with a plain weave. It is crisper than batiste, but not as crisp as organdie.

Mercerised cotton. A strong, lustrous fabric that is easy to dye and is resistant to mildew. Tension is applied to the fabric, which is then saturated with a cold caustic soda solution that is later neutralised. The fibre swells permanently, increasing the lustre and making it easier to apply other finishes. The process was discovered by accident and patented by John Mercer in England in 1844.

Organdy or Organdie. A very light, sheer, cotton fabric with a plain weave of tightly twisted fibres and a mercerised finish added to give it a characteristic crispness.

Organza. A very light, sheer, stiff fabric similar to organdy but made of silk or man-made fibre yarns.

Pima cotton. This is used to make fine knitted goods and expensive woven fabrics. The best Pima cottons are Egyptian, Sea Island and the US Southwest high-grade cotton.

Piqué. A light to heavy weight cotton fabric with a raised woven design, usually on the warp threads. Piqué has more body than flat fabrics.

Plissé. A lightweight cotton or cotton blend fabric printed with a chemical solution in the form of stripes. The chemical shrinks areas of the fabric, causing the untreated parts to pucker. Plissé has the appearance of seersucker with the crinkled fabric being less structured.

Ramie. A natural fibre fabric made from the nettle plant. Similar in character to handkerchief linen, ramie has more lustre than linen and can be woven into fabric as fine as imported Swiss batiste.

Seersucker. A firmly woven fabric with lengthwise puckered stripes. The stripes are made by adjusting the tension on the weaving loom, causing the slack fibres to pucker permanently. Seersucker can be sheer or heavy, and woven with a solid colour or dyed yarns to produce stripes or checks.

Swiss batiste. A sheer, transparent fabric with a high lustre, which is achieved by a special finish and the use of special grades of long staple cotton and Swiss mercerisation.

Voile. A semi-sheer, dainty fabric made with tightly twisted yarns and a loose plain weave, usually with the same number of yarns in both directions.

Fabric terminology

Bias   An oblique direction to the warp and the weft. The true bias is at an angle of 45° from both the warp and weft threads. The bias grain has the most 'memory' and is also known as cutting on the cross.

Cross Grain   The direction of the weft threads across the fabric perpendicular to the selvedges.

Grain   The direction of the lengthwise or warp threads, parallel to the selvedges. These are the strongest, most stable threads.

Selvedges   These are the reinforced edges of the fabric. Current manufacturing techniques ensure the selvedge is closely woven. Trim it away before cutting the pattern pieces or preparing a width of fabric for pleating and smocking.

Warp and weft threads   The names for the two sets of threads that are required for the manufacture of woven fabrics. **Warp** threads run along the fabric length, parallel to the selvedge. **Weft** threads run across the fabric width, from selvedge to selvedge.

Interfacing

When constructing a garment, interfacing can be applied to the wrong side of the fabric pieces to provide shape and stability.

Interfacings are available in light, medium and heavy weights and can be stitched or fused to the fabric. They may be woven or non-woven, and made from natural or synthetic fibres.

Sew-in interfacing is tacked or basted to the fabric piece. It is suitable where heat or pressure from fusing would damage the garment fabric, or where the garment fabric is so sheer, the bonding agent would seep through.

Fusible interfacing has a fusing agent on one side, which melts and adheres when heat and pressure is applied. Effective fusing requires a specific amount of heat, moisture, pressure and time. Always follow the manufacturer's instructions carefully to avoid puckering.

Woven interfacings are usually cut with the grain matching the grain of the fabric piece. They can be fusible or sew-in.

Non-woven interfacings have no grain and can be cut in any direction.

Pre-shrinking interfacing

Shrinkage after construction of either the fabric or the interfacing, is the single most common problem. To avoid this, always choose an interfacing that matches the care requirements of your fabric and pre-shrink the interfacing if recommended by the manufacturer.

Sew-in interfacings can be pre-shrunk in the same way as you would care for the finished garment. A washable interfacing can be steam shrunk by holding a steaming iron 5cm (2") above the interfacing, to maintain the crispness or if the fabric to which it will be applied is 'dry-clean only'.

Fusible interfacings have very different shrinkage rates depending on how the interfacing is constructed. Preshrink woven or knit interfacings by placing them into warm or hot water for 15 minutes or until the water cools to room temperature. Pour out the water and gently squeeze out excess. Take care not to wring the interfacing, since it cannot be ironed before use. Open out and leave to dry flat or over a clothes airer.

The interfacing should always be the same weight or lighter than the garment fabric. For fine heirloom sewing, a lightweight woven cotton fusible interfacing is recommended. For sheer fabrics, where the interfacing may show through, an additional piece of the garment fabric is a good alternative to interfacing.

Machine sewing threads

Choosing the correct thread for an heirloom project is just as important as choosing the fabric and trims.

When working with lace, entredeux and fabric on an heirloom project, the thread colour should usually match the lace or entredeux. In cases where the securing zigzag stitches will be visible on the right side, match the thread colour to the fabric.

Machine threads are available in various fibres and weights. For best results use cotton thread on natural fibre fabrics and always use the same thread on both the top spool and in the bobbin for correct tension.

Thread size or weight is expressed as a number, the higher the number, the finer the thread. Some cotton threads have a second number, eg 60/2, which indicates the number of plies used to make the thread.

Fine weight threads made especially for fine or heirloom sewing make the stitches less visible. The stitch length, not the weight of the thread, determines the strength of a fabric seam or join.

Cotona 80, Lacis 120 or Tanne 80 are suitable for techniques where there is a build-up of threads such as hemstitch or zigzag.

DMC 50 or Mettler 60/2 are recommended for embroidery or close zigzag stitching and garment construction using fine fabrics.

Cotona 50, DMC 30, Mettler 50/3 or Coats and Clark's dual duty extra fine threads are used for garment construction of medium-weight fabrics.

Notions

Notions are the additional items you need to finish your project.

Fasteners

Buttons are available in an infinite number of styles, sizes, shapes and colours. When choosing one that is right for the garment, keep in mind that novelty buttons with sharp or odd angles, may not be a suitable or practical form of closure and are best used as decoration only.

Fabric covered buttons provide a suitable alternative when the perfect ready-made button cannot be found.

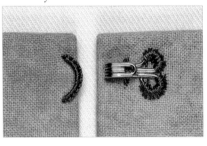

Hooks and eyes are small two-part fasteners made from metal. They are used to invisibly hold opening edges that are butted together. An alternative to the metal eye is to stitch a blanket stitch loop.

Snap fasteners are made from clear plastic or metal and consist of a ball section that fits into a socket section. For fine heirloom garments metal snap fasteners can be covered with the garment fabric to produce a true vintage appearance.

Ribbons and braids

Ribbons are available in an array of widths, colours, patterns and textures. In heirloom sewing, satin and silk ribbons are used to decorate garments, often threaded through entredeux or beading lace.

Ricrac is a firmly woven cotton trim that forms a zigzag effect. Available in several widths and a variety of colours it can be used to trim collars, yokes and hem lines or shaped for decorative designs.

Trims

One of the characteristics of heirloom sewing is the extensive use of trims such as lace and entredeux. When selecting trims make sure they suit the weight of your fabric and the size of the garment.

Before commencing work with lace or embroideries, mist the pieces with water and press with steam to ensure they hold their shape once stitched.

Beading is a lace or embroidered insertion, edging, or galloon with small holes along the centre through which ribbon may be woven or threaded.

Broderie anglaise is a form of white embroidery, which is characterized by eyelet holes surrounded by buttonhole stitches.

Cordonnet is a distinct, heavier thread that outlines the design in a lace.

Ditch is a sewing term referring to the seamline joining two fabric pieces. In heirloom sewing this term also refers to the straight edge of the embroidery on beading or entredeux

Edging refers to lace or embroidery that has a decorative edge along one side and a heading of plain fabric along the other side, to which the fabric is attached.

Entredeux loosely translated means 'between two'. Entredeux is a 3–12mm wide (⅛–½") embroidered veining, stitched on cotton batiste to create a ladder effect. It is used to secure or enhance a seam or join.

Galloon refers to lace, embroidery or embroidered eyelet with a decorative edge on both sides. It can range from 12mm–25cm (½–10") in width.

Gimp thread is the outermost thread along the lace heading. It is usually slightly looped and is the first thread pulled when shaping or gathering lace.

Handloom is a term for fabrics or trims which are woven on either the hand or hand-and-foot power loom. These are now rarely made and difficult to find.

Heading is a firm band of threads along the straight edges of a lace.

Insertion is a band of lace, eyelet or embroidery with two straight edges that can be set into fabric. Embroidery or embroidered beading is also known as Swiss insertion.

Lace is fine netting or open-work fabric of linen, cotton or silk, It is produced by stitching, interlacing or twisting threads in several directions to produce a porous trim. This can be an insertion or edging.

Medallion is an oval or circular design resembling a medal in shape, made of lace or embroidery and used as decoration on a garment.

Ruche is a strip of pleated or frilled fabric or ribbon used as a decorative edging.

Swiss edging refers to embroidery that is worked on fine batiste to form a decorative stitched edge on one side and plain fabric on the other, to allow it to be attached to the garment. Although the finest qualities are Swiss, other embroideries of this style come from Asia and Eastern Europe.

Lace

Alençon lace is a light hexagonal mesh net ground developed in the French region of Alençon during the mid 18th century. It is a slow and difficult lace to produce, making it expensive to purchase.

Baby lace is a general term referring to light narrow lace edging or insertion not more than 1cm (⅜") wide.

Binche is a very fine cotton straight-edge lace, characterised by a spotted design. Originally handmade in Flanders, machine made reproductions are readily available.

Bobbin lace is a general term describing handmade lace made with bobbins on a special lace making pillow or bolster. Following a pricked pattern, pins are inserted into the pillow while the lace is being made, to keep all the thread crossings in place until that lace portion is secure. Hand-made Valenciennes, Binche, Mechlin, Chantilly and Honiton are some examples of bobbin lace.

Cluny is a coarse, strong cotton lace with a geometric design. It was formerly made by hand in France and Belgium from linen thread.

Filet lace is a needle made lace formed with square meshes partially filled in to create a design. It is also the name given to crochet lace of similar design.

Irish crochet lace is a cotton lace made by crocheting to form characteristic designs with picoted brides.

Limerick is a delicate lace embroidered by hand in a variety of stitches onto fine cotton net. This lace is well suited for collars, cuffs and medallions.

Maline was originally made by hand in Maline, Belgium. It is an open textured diamond shaped fine mesh with small, pretty floral designs. Motifs on the mesh background are hand trimmed.

Mechlin is a bobbin lace mesh of very fine thread. Early Mechlin lace had a six-sided mesh ground. However, present day Mechlin lace is often found with diamond shaped ground. It is usually characterised by floral motifs with a fine cordonnet. It is lighter in weight than Alençon but as strong as Valenciennes.

Picot lace is an edging with narrow, triangular or rounded loops along the outer edge.

Tatting is a lace made by looping and knotting a thread that is wound onto a hand shuttle.

Valenciennes lace or Val is a fine cotton bobbin lace usually with a hexagonal or diamond shaped mesh background, originally made by hand and later by machine in Valenciennes, France. French Val lace is the most widely used lace in fine hand or machine sewing.

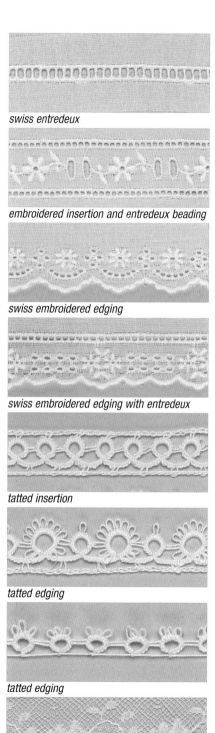

swiss entredeux

embroidered insertion and entredeux beading

swiss embroidered edging

swiss embroidered edging with entredeux

tatted insertion

tatted edging

tatted edging

french valenciennes picot lace edging

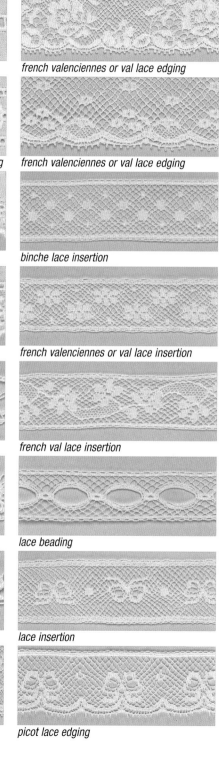

french valenciennes or val lace edging

french valenciennes or val lace edging

binche lace insertion

french valenciennes or val lace insertion

french val lace insertion

lace beading

lace insertion

picot lace edging

General instructions

Preparation

Preparing fabrics

Fabric preparation is essential before you start cutting. When buying your fabric, take note of the care requirements. If the fabric has been folded on a bolt, check to ensure the foldlines have not faded and can be pressed out when required.

It is not imperative that you launder the fabric before use if you are using good quality fabrics. However, cheaper fabrics are often treated with large amounts of sizing or starch to make them crisp, and these most definitely need laundering before you begin sewing.

Following the manufacturer's instructions, pre-shrink fabrics that may shrink when laundered.

Hold the fabric up the light to see if there are any holes or flaws that should be avoided. If you find any, mark them and ensure they are avoided when you position the pattern pieces.

Preparing trims

It is recommended that you preshrink laces, insertions and entredeux by misting with water and pressing with steam. This will ensure they hold their shape once stitched. Spray starch is only required for pressing before cutting out if several components have been joined to create an heirloom fabric.

Cutting out

The grain on which a pattern piece is cut affects the way a garment hangs or drapes. It is very important that you always cut your garment in the direction indicated by the grainline arrows on each pattern piece.

The warp or lengthwise grain is the strongest and has very little give or stretch. In most garments this hangs vertically, taking the weight of the garment from shoulder to hem.

The weft or crosswise grain is more pliable and drapes differently, giving the garment a softer appearance.

The bias grain has the most stretch, allowing it to drape softly. A bias cut skirt or dress should be hung and left until the sections with the greatest stretch have dropped to their lowest level before the hem is straightened and finished.

Right and wrong side

It can at times be difficult to determine the right and wrong sides of a fabric. Smooth fabrics usually have a delicate sheen on the right side and appear dull on the wrong side.

When there is no apparent difference between the right and wrong sides, choose one and mark this side on all garment pieces with clear tape or a marking pencil.

Laying out the fabric

Work on the largest surface available. It should be long enough to accommodate the full length of the fabric wherever possible. It is advisable not to disturb the layout until you have cut out all the pieces. Determine how the fabric should be folded and ensure both layers are perfectly aligned. For fabrics that shift easily, pin the selvedges together at short intervals along the length.

Pattern pieces

Identify all the pattern pieces needed for the chosen garment and check the pattern measurements against those of

Straightening the fabric

Very few pieces of fabric have both selvedges and grainlines perfectly aligned and at right angles to each other. To achieve the correct alignment, cut the upper and lower edges following a thread in the weave. Cut either by sight or by pulling a weft thread until it breaks and cutting along the pulled thread. At the break point pick up another thread and continue with the *pull-and-cut* method for cutting a straight line.

To square the fabric and straighten the grain, fold the fabric in half along the length, matching the selvedges and the upper cut edge. Hold up the length and check if the selvedges stay aligned.

If they remain aligned or there is very little difference you can proceed to lay it out and cut out the garment pieces.

A greater difference in the way the selvedges hang may be corrected by pressing with steam.

the wearer. Consider any style changes you wish to make, such as eliminating trims or reshaping collars.

Carefully press out any creases from the pattern pieces. Trace the pattern pieces onto tracing paper or non-woven interfacing to preserve the original. Alter the pattern if necessary, ensuring that the alterations are visible on both sides and that the same alterations have been marked on all corresponding pieces. The length of the garment should be checked and altered if necessary before cutting out.

Marking the fabric

Transferring markings from the pattern to your cut fabric is important to ensure the best result.

There is a variety of tools and techniques used for transferring pattern markings onto fabric. Choose the method suitable for your fabric and the sewing techniques you will be using. In most cases a combination of marking methods will work best. Test your marking method on a small piece of fabric to determine its suitability.

Transfer the pattern markings after the garment pieces have been cut out. Where possible always transfer the pattern markings onto the wrong side of both fabric layers.

Tailor's chalk or chalk marking pencil is suitable for temporary marks.

Water-soluble fabric marker is suitable for temporary marks or where the marks will be removed by cutting. It is essential that the fabric is not pressed until after the marks are removed as heat will make them permanent.

Fading marker or pencil can be used for temporary marks. However, always test before using.

Thread tracing or tacking is time consuming, but is invaluable for fabrics unsuitable for other forms of marking or for long-term projects. Lines of tacking can be used to mark the centre front or back lines, fold lines or the roll line of a collar. Use a light coloured contrasting thread and avoid tacking along stitchlines as the tacking may become caught in the stitching.

Templates

It is a good idea to prepare a template for shapes such as hearts, diamonds, teardrops, scalloped hems and edges.

Draw or trace the shape and any placement marks onto firm card and cut out, ensuring the edges are smooth.

Making a scallop template

Measure the finished width or circumference of the hem on which the scalloped hem will be. Divide this measurement by a suitable scallop width for the size of the project. This gives you the number of scallops that will fit across the width.

Rule a line equal to the depth of the hem on a piece of card. This is the scallop placement line. Mark the width of the scallops along this line, for the positions of the points. Two or three scallops is usually sufficient on one template.

Determine a suitable depth for the scallops, keeping in mind that shallow scallops are easier to turn neatly and smoothly than deeper scallops. For 15cm (6") wide scallops, a depth of 3.5cm (1⅜") usually works well.

Using a curved tool such as a memory curve or a scallop radial rule, draw the scallops along the placement line. Kitchen implements, such as pot lids and plates with a curve that fits the desired width and depth are also useful for drawing curves.

Cut out the scallop template, ensuring the edges are smooth.

Seams

To achieve even, smooth seams always hold the work taut from both sides of the presser foot. Avoid pulling the fabric but keep an even tension allowing it to feed under the presser foot.

Starting and finishing

To avoid the bulk of back stitching, start and finish each seam using a very short stitch length, (0.5–0.75) for the distance of the seam allowance. This method allows for a single, yet secure, row of stitches at the beginning and end of each row.

Always hold both the top and bobbin threads behind the presser foot as you commence stitching to prevent the fabrics being pulled into the bobbin casing. This is particularly important when working with lace and entredeux.

Grading

After stitching, seam allowances may need to be graded to reduce bulk. Trim the layers of the seam allowance to different widths, leaving the widest to sit nearest the garment. This ensures the seam will not cause ridges when pressed.

Staystitch

A line of stitching to stabilise the fabric and prevent unwanted stretching prior to seaming along curved or bias edges. It is usually placed no more than 2mm (¹⁄₁₆") inside the stitchline within the seam allowance using a short straight stitch.

Topstitch

Topstitching creates a decorative finish as well as reinforcing a seam.

1   Stitch, set and grade the seam. From the wrong side press the seam allowance towards the side, to be topstitched, pushing against the stitchline with the side of the iron. Roll and finger press the seamline so it sits just to the underside.
2   With the right side uppermost, stitch an even distance from the seamline or finished edge. Use a reference point on the presser foot or an edge-joining foot as a guide.

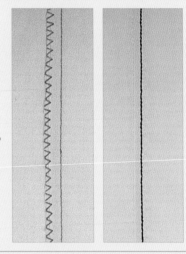

Gathering

As a general rule, more gathering rows are better than less, to achieve even gathers.

When gathering fine fabrics use a short gathering stitch length (2.5–3.5). This length will cause the fine fabric to gather gently, whereas a longer stitch will cause the fabric to pleat. Once the gathering rows are stitched, isolate the bobbin threads at each end and tie them together in a knot. This ensures that you always draw up the bobbin threads in one movement.

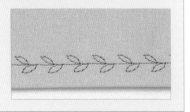

Underststitching

This helps to prevent an inner part of a garment, such as a facing or lining, from rolling to the outside.

After grading and clipping the seam allowance, press the facing or lining away from the garment, onto the seam allowance. With the right side facing, stitch close to the seam through all layers of the lining and seam allowance.

Pressing

Pressing is an essential part of good garment construction. It is important to understand the difference between pressing and ironing.

Ironing is the process of moving the iron backwards and forwards to remove wrinkles or smooth out the fabric.

Pressing involves very little movement of the iron, applying more pressure in certain areas. The iron is moved in an up and down motion, using the steam to set the stitches, seams or shapes and curves. Pressing is carried out at every step during the construction process. Always press each seam or section before it is crossed by another. Press on the wrong side or use a pressing cloth to protect the right side from iron shine.

Setting the stitches or melding

Press the stitchline with steam to settle the stitches into the fibres of the fabric. Always press to set the stitches along each seam before pressing the seam open or attaching another part of the garment.

Using spray starch

Use a good quality spray starch and rinse the nozzle regularly to prevent clogging. Apply one or two light mists of spray starch and allow the starch to soak into the fabric before pressing. Avoid saturating the fabric, to prevent starch build-up on the iron sole plate.

Your finished project

Considering the treatment heirloom garments received when less was known about the stress of laundering and the pitfalls of storage, it is surprising that so many have survived.

Incorrect laundering and storage is generally what damages a garment, not the wearing. With that in mind the following information will assist with the correct care for preserving these special garments.

Any fabric that is crushed or tightly folded will deteriorate more quickly along the crease lines. Frequent and rough handling can cause damage by introducing dirt and perspiration between the

fibres. Other destructive factors include frequent exposure to sunlight, storage conditions that are too dry or too moist and atmospheric pollution, especially in city areas. Not completely rinsing laundry detergent or starch, or storing with the garment touching the sides of a wooden chest can also cause damage to the fibres.

Laundering

Detergent

Modern laundry detergents contain bleaching agents that cause deterioration in the fibres of the fabric. Stain removers should be used with great care using a pressing action, as rubbing the stain will damage the fabric.

Choose a good quality mild washing powder that contains no bleaching agent or enzymes.

Washing

Garments should be hand washed to prevent stress on delicate lace and embroideries. Should you choose to machine wash, select a gentle cycle and place the garment in a mesh bag.

Dissolve the washing powder thoroughly in warm water. Submerge the garment fully and leave it to soak for hours if necessary. Avoid scrubbing or agitating the garment, just swish and squeeze the garment occasionally to move the water through.

If the garment is heavily soiled, use a fresh washing powder solution and repeat the process.

Rinse the garment well in warm water, gently squeezing the water through the fabric until it is clear. Handle the garment carefully and do not twist or wring. Rinse in cold water for the final rinse to help reduce creases.

It is important that the detergent is thoroughly rinsed from the garment, as any residue left in the fibres can continue to act on the fibres and may scorch when pressed.

Let the excess water drain out before lifting the garment.

Drying

Spread the garment on a towel or sheet and roll up firmly. Press gently to remove excess water, but do not wring or twist.

Lay the garment flat on an absorbent covering. Place tulle or clear plastic bags inside the sleeves and bodice to help smooth out creases. Gently smooth out laces, tucks and frills while the garment is wet. This will help when it comes to ironing the garment.

It is not advisable to place a garment on a hanger or over a rack to dry as this will cause it to stretch and leave marks from the hanger and rack. Take care not to pull at any laces as they tear very easily when wet.

Iron the garment before it is completely dry if possible.

Ironing

Ensure all traces of pattern markings are removed before you iron. Press the garment, avoiding any smocking and other raised or textured areas. Always use a pressing cloth to protect the fabric surface when pressing from the right side.

If a garment needs to be starched, use a good quality starch and follow the instructions. However, the starch must be thoroughly rinsed from the garment before storing.

Sequence of pressing

Press sleeves and sleeve bands first, using the sleeve roll or a pressing mitt to eliminate all creases. Pack the sleeves with tissue paper or tulle to maintain their shape. Press collars from the underside. If the collar is embroidered, press into a soft surface to avoid crushing the embroidery. For the final press on collars, try finger pressing to avoid pressing in ridges or making impressions. Press the front yoke and back bodices taking care around buttons. Press the skirt, pushing the iron as far up into any gathers or pleats as possible. Finally press sashes and ties.

Hanging

Leave the tissue paper or tulle inside the sleeves to prevent them from becoming crushed. Leave sashes untied. Place the garment onto a padded hanger and hang in a well aired position.

Storage

Heirloom garments often need to be stored for many years.

Always be sure garments are spotlessly clean before storing them. Soils attract insects and body stains can discolour and permanently stain and weaken the fabric. Materials such as cardboard or wood that touch garments in storage also affect their colour and condition.

Press the garment without using spray starch to eliminate creases that can cause deterioration.

Hanging

Garments should never be stored in plastic bags, as these can induce high humidity levels, leaving damp patches on the material that may cause mildew stains.

Hang the garment on padded hangers, filling puffed sleeves with acid-free tissue paper or tulle. Cover the garment with a lightweight cotton bag or dust cover. Before making the cotton dust cover, launder the fabric several times in hot water to remove the starch or sizing. Rinse well. Cotton dust covers create no static electricity to attract dust and can be laundered periodically.

Storage boxes

As an alternative, garments can be surrounded in white acid-free tissue paper and stored flat in acid-free boxes. Prepare a clean box that is large enough to hold the items with as little folding as possible. If some folding is necessary, place tissue paper over the garment before folding. Fold loosely over the paper, avoiding any sharp creases. Each item should be loosely layered with tissue paper to support the article and then more tissue paper placed over the surface to protect it. It is essential that you use crushed tissue paper to stuff and retain the shape of certain parts of the garment. Avoid placing too many items into one box.

The box should be labelled and stored out of sunlight, ideally at a constant temperature and humidity. This is not always possible outside of museum conditions so reasonable care must be taken to keep the articles clean, boxed and away from heat, damp and sunlight if they are to be preserved for future generations.

Periodically examine the garments in storage to control infestations of insects such as clothes moth, carpet beetle, silverfish etc. Vacuum the storage area regularly to reduce this possibility. If necessary, lightly vacuum a garment through a covered nozzle to protect fabric, lace and trims.

Garment records

If you have ever pondered the previous life of an antique garment in your possession then consider adding a photograph and document the garment you have created. Photograph the baby being baptised in your christening gown, adding names, birth and christening details afterwards.

Entredeux techniques

The extensive use of entredeux is the one of the most significant elements of heirloom sewing. It can be used as a design feature between laces, between fabric and lace, as a foundation for other trims and finishes or for strengthening parts of a garment. The right side of the entredeux is more rounded than the wrong side.

ADJUSTING MACHINE SETTINGS

It is important to test your machine settings before commencing any work using entredeux. The width of the zigzag stitch should encompass the embroidered edge of the entredeux and the stitch length adjusted to place a stitch into each hole.

Your zigzag machine settings will become out of synchronisation with the entredeux holes from time to time. To correct, lift the presser foot and reposition the needle to continue with the correct sequence.

Preparation. Cut a piece of entredeux 10cm (4") long. Do not trim the entredeux headings. Lightly spray with water and press with steam to shrink the batiste heading.

Suggested machine settings

Zigzag stitch
W: 2.5, L: 1.0
Presser foot: edge-joining
Needle position: centre

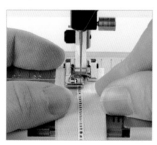

1 Hold the entredeux taut from both sides of the presser foot. Begin with the needle in one of the entredeux holes.

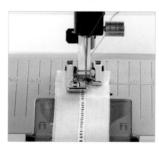

2 Begin to stitch very slowly. The right needle swing will be positioned on the batiste heading.

3 Stitch carefully, ensuring the needle goes into a new hole with each left swing. Adjust the machine settings as required.

Hint

Sewing entredeux

Hold the entredeux firmly with the thumb in front and a finger behind the presser foot, but avoid stretching or pulling it. Imagine the entredeux feeding under the foot like a piece of cardboard. If the zigzag misses a hole, the fabric and thread will not be dragged into the bobbin casing when you are holding it firmly.

JOINING ENTREDEUX

When entredeux is stitched to a neatened edge joined by a seam, such as a sleeve, the ends will need to be overlapped and secured by hand. Always complete the garment seams first.

Preparation. Stitch the seam and roll and whip the raw edge. Trim the heading from one side of the entredeux.

1 Starting at the seam and leaving 1cm (⅜") extending, stitch the entredeux to the fabric by hand or machine.

2 When reaching the seam, trim any excess entredeux, leaving two holes overlapping.

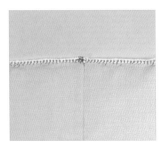

3 Trim the remaining entredeux heading. Overcast stitch the outer edge and the bars of the overlapped section together.

4 End off by weaving the thread through the previous stitches and trim the tail. Press the entredeux away from the fabric.

TRIMMING ENTREDEUX

With seam allowance

When working on a garment with a specific seam allowance, wherever possible trim the seam allowance and entredeux heading to the same measurement. This will allow you to match the raw edges so you do not have to accommodate varying seam allowances.

TRIMMING ENTREDEUX

Without seam allowance

For some techniques the batiste heading will need to be cut away before stitching. The entredeux is more stable if you remove the heading as you are about to stitch.

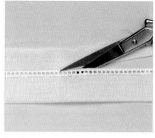

1 Cut away the batiste heading along the side that is to be stitched. On long lengths, cut a small section at a time.

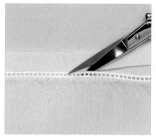

2 Stitch the trimmed entredeux edge in place using your chosen method. Cut away the remaining heading.

ATTACHING ENTREDEUX TO ENTREDEUX

Two or more pieces of entredeux can be joined to form a wider trim.

1 With the right sides facing, trim the heading from one side of each piece of entredeux.

2 Butt two trimmed edges together.

3 Stitch, ensuring the needle swings into each hole of both pieces of entredeux.

4 Trim the remaining heading from one piece of entredeux.

5 Attach the next piece of entredeux in the same manner.

ATTACHING ENTREDEUX TO FABRIC

By hand

This is the traditional method of attaching entredeux and results in an almost invisible seam.

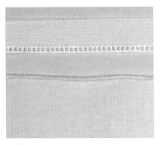

1 Prepare the fabric with a rolled and whipped edge using your chosen method. Trim the heading from one side of the entredeux.

2 With right sides together match the trimmed edge of the entredeux with the neatened fabric edge. Slide the needle behind the rolled edge and emerge through a hole in the entredeux.

3 Pull the thread through. Take the needle from back to front. Slide the needle behind the roll and emerge through the next hole in the entredeux.

4 Continue stitching the entredeux to the rolled and whipped edge in this manner. Secure the thread in the roll of the fabric.

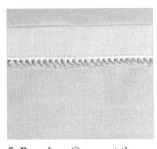

5 **Pressing**. Open out the fabric and entredeux. With the wrong side facing, gently press the rolled seam away from the entredeux using the side of the iron. The holes will be clearly visible.

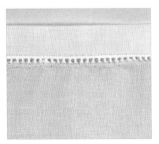

6 Turn to the right and press again to set the seam away from the entredeux holes.

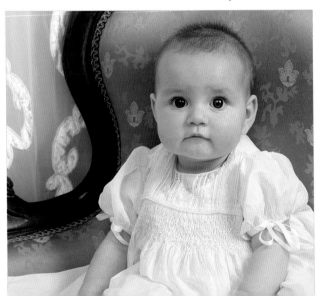

ATTACHING ENTREDEUX TO FABRIC

By machine *method one*

This method creates the strongest and most stable join. It leaves the full width of the embroidered entredeux beading free without visible stitches on the front. Test and adjust your machine settings to suit your entredeux. The left needle swing should go into the ditch and the right needle swing should clear the raw edge of the seam allowance to roll the seam.

Preparation. Trim the seam allowances of the entredeux heading and fabric piece to the same measurement.

Suggested machine settings

Straight stitch	*Zigzag stitch*
L: 2.0	W: 2.5–3.0, L: 0.75–1.5
Presser foot: edge-joining	Presser foot: edge-joining
Needle position: centre	Needle position: far right

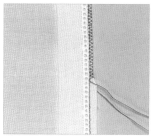

1 Place the entredeux over the fabric with right sides together and matching raw edges. Stitch in the ditch of the entredeux using a small straight stitch.

2 Trim the seam allowance of the fabric and entredeux to 3mm (⅛").

3 Ensuring the left needle swing goes into the ditch, zigzag the seam allowances together with a fine rolled seam, covering the previous stitchline. The zigzag will encase the fabric edge and cause a tight roll.

4 **Pressing.** Open out the fabric and entredeux. With the wrong side facing, gently press the rolled seam away from the entredeux using the side of the iron.

5 Turn to the right side and press again to set the seam away from the entredeux holes. The holes will be clearly visible.

Hint

Needle position

On some machines it is not possible to move the needle position in zigzag mode. Use the embroidery or basic presser foot and the centre needle position.

ATTACHING ENTREDEUX TO FABRIC

By machine *method two*

Thais method is stitched into the entredeux holes to create a durable seam. The entredeux holes sit against the fabric edge when the seam is pressed back. Test and adjust your zigzag stitch to suit your entredeux before you begin.

Suggested machine settings

Zigzag stitch
W: 2.5–3.0, L: 0.75–1.0
Presser foot: edge-joining or all-purpose
Needle position: far right

1 Roll and whip the edge of the fabric following the instructions on page 42.

2 Trim the heading from one side of the entredeux. With right sides together, align the trimmed edge of the entredeux with the neatened fabric edge.

3 Zigzag slowly, ensuring the left needle swing goes into each hole of the entredeux and the right needle swing clears the rolled fabric edge.

4 Adjust the stitch settings as required to ensure the stitches clear the entredeux bars.

5 **Pressing.** Open out the fabric and entredeux. With the wrong side facing, gently press the rolled seam away from the entredeux using the side of the iron.

6 Turn to the right and press again to set the fabric away from the entredeux holes. The holes will be clearly visible.

ATTACHING ENTREDEUX TO GATHERED FABRIC

This method creates a strong and stable join.
Preparation. Trim the entredeux heading and garment seam allowance to the same measurement. Mark the half and quarter points on both the entredeux and the fabric.

1 Using a contrasting thread, stitch the first row of machine gathering just outside the stitchline.

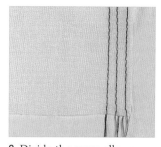

2 Divide the seam allowance into thirds and stitch two more rows of gathering.

Suggested machine settings

Gathering straight stitch
L: 3.0–3.5
Presser foot: edge-joining
Needle position: centre

Zigzag stitch
W: 2.0–2.5
L: 0.75–1.5
Presser foot: edge-joining or all-purpose
Needle position: centre

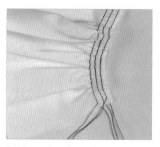

3 Knot the three bobbin threads together at each end. Gently pull the bobbin threads and gather the fabric from each end to the required measurement.

4 With right sides together and matching marks, pin and tack the entredeux to the gathered edge. The first row of gathering will be visible through the entredeux holes.

5 With the entredeux uppermost, stitch in the ditch of the entredeux using a short straight stitch.

6 Gently press the stitches with the tip of the iron, taking care to press on the seam allowance only.

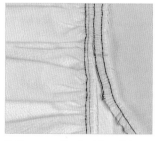

7 Remove the tacking. Trim and grade the seam allowance of the gathered fabric to no less than 1.5mm (¹⁄₁₆") and the entredeux heading to 3mm (⅛").

8 Slowly zigzag a fine rolled seam, encasing the previous stitchline. Ensure the left needle swing goes into the ditch of the entredeux and the right needle swing clears the rolled fabric edge.

ATTACHING ENTREDEUX TO A CONCAVE CURVE

This technique creates a firm and neat finish for a neckline or the armholes of a petticoat. It can be further embellished with lace or a hand worked trim.

Preparation. Neaten the curved fabric using your chosen method. Test and adjust your stitch settings to suit your entredeux.

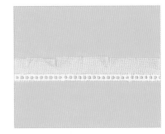

1 Trim the batiste heading from one side of the entredeux. Trim the remaining heading to 6mm (¼") and clip at 6mm (¼") intervals.

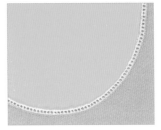

2 With the right side facing, shape and press the entredeux to match thecurved edge to which it will be attached. Lightly mist with spray starch and press again.

3 With right sides facing, lay the edge of the entredeux against the neatened fabric edge. Carefully zigzag the edges together, stitching into each hole of the entredeux and over the rolled fabric edge.

4 **Finishing.** Carefully trim the remaining heading. Sample stitched using matching thread.

ATTACHING ENTREDEUX TO A CONVEX CURVE

Entredeux can be used as a subtle finish to a scalloped hemline or the outer edge of a round or Peter Pan collar. The entredeux can be further embellished with lace or a hand worked trim.

It is important that you apply ample ease to the entredeux when you attach it to a convex curve. Even the slightest stretch on the entredeux will cause the fabric curve to pucker.

Preparation. Neaten the curved fabric edge using your chosen method. Test and adjust your stitch settings to suit your entredeux.

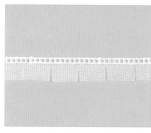

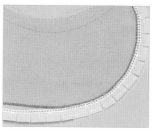

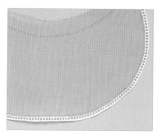

1 Trim the batiste heading from one side of the entredeux. Trim the remaining batiste heading to 6mm (¼") and clip at 6mm (¼") intervals.

2 With the right side facing, shape and press the entredeux to match the curved edge to which it will be attached. Lightly mist with spray starch and press again.

3 With right sides facing, lay the edge of the entredeux against the prepared fabric edge. Zigzag the edges together, stitching into each hole of the entredeux and over the rolled fabric edge.

4 Finishing. Carefully trim the remaining heading. Sample stitched using matching thread.

ATTACHING ENTREDEUX TO A CORNER

Single fabric thickness

This method is used for applying entredeux, Swiss beading or insertion to the edge of a single fabric thickness such as a handkerchief or the mitred hemline of a Christening gown.

Preparation. Cut each length of entredeux, 12mm (½") longer than the fabric edge at each corner. Trim the batiste heading from one side of the entredeux.

1 Trim the remaining entredeux heading to 6mm (¼") or to match the seam allowance of the fabric.

2 Mark the corner point with a small dot. Matching raw edges, position the entredeux along one side of the fabric and pin in place, leaving 12mm (½") extending beyond the fabric edge.

3 Repeat for the adjacent side. Where the two lengths of entredeux overlap, trim the remaining headings back to the corner point.

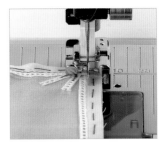

4 To avoid catching the entredeux tails at the corner point, fold them back onto the fabric. Tack in place.

5 Straight stitch in the ditch of the entredeux. Shorten the stitch length when nearing the corner.

6 Stop at the corner point with the needle in the fabric only. Lift the presser foot and pivot.

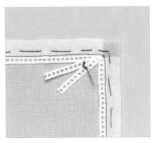

7 Continue to stitch along the adjacent side.

8 Remove the tacking. Trim the seam allowance to 3mm (⅛"). Keeping the entredeux tails out of the way, zigzag a fine rolled seam along one side at a time. Do not pivot at the corner.

9 Roll and press the seams towards the fabric.

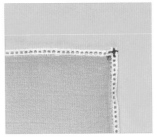

10 Working from the right side, align the two corner holes of the entredeux. Handstitch together using very small stitches and fine thread.

11 Trim the entredeux tails to form a neat corner. The corner is now ready to attach a ruffle, lace edging or hand embellishment.

12 Entredeux attached with matching thread and finished with a gathered lace edging.

ATTACHING ENTREDEUX TO A CORNER

Between fabric layers

This method is suitable for applying entredeux, Swiss beading or insertion to the edge of a square collar, pillowslip, quilt or cot cover.

Preparation. Cut each length of entredeux, 12mm (½") longer than the fabric edge at each corner. Trim the batiste heading from one side of the entredeux.

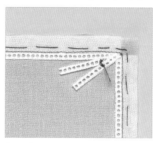

1 Following steps 1–7 on pages 33–34, stitch the entredeux to the lining or back piece.

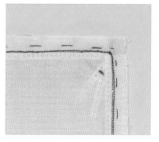

2 Matching raw edges, tack the front to the back, sandwiching the entredeux between. Stitch just inside the previous stitchline, pivoting on the previous pivot point.

3 Gently press this stitchline to set the seam. Grade the seam allowances so that the widest seam allowance is towards the front. Trim across the corner.

4 Turn to the right side. Align the corner holes and handstitch together. Trim the entredeux tails.

ATTACHING ENTREDEUX TO FLAT LACE

Take care not to pull or put any pressure on the lace while stitching, as this will create ripples in the lace. Hold the entredeux taut and allow the lace to feed through the machine.

Preparation. Test and adjust the zigzag stitch to suit your entredeux and lace before you begin. If the zigzag is too wide it will bite into the lace design causing distortion.

1 Lightly mist the lace and entredeux pieces with water. Press and steam. Trim the heading from one side of the entredeux.

2 With right sides facing, lay the trimmed edge of the entredeux against the lace heading. Position the pieces under the presser foot.

Hint

Left handed sewers

This method works well for right-handed sewers because they can hold the entredeux taut between the thumb and third finger of the left hand, while controlling the lace with the right hand. Left-handed sewers might find it more comfortable to attach the lace from the other side.

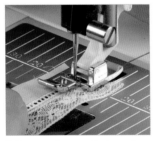

3 Lower the needle into the first entredeux hole. Hold the threads and entredeux taut.

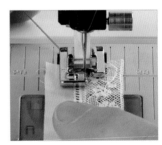

4 Begin to stitch slowly, ensuring the left needle swing goes into each hole of the entredeux and the right needle swing just clears the lace heading.

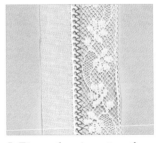

5 Zigzag the pieces together slowly. Re-adjust the stitches as required to maintain correct sequence.

ATTACHING ENTREDEUX TO GATHERED LACE

Control the entredeux and lace in a similar manner as when stitching entredeux to flat lace.

Preparation. Test and adjust the zigzag stitch to suit your entredeux and lace before you begin. If the zigzag is too wide it will bite into the lace design causing distortion.

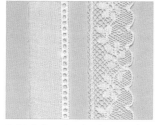

1 Lightly mist the lace and entredeux pieces with water. Press and steam. Trim one heading from the entredeux.

Suggested machine settings

Zigzag stitch
W: 2.0–2.5, L: 0.75–1.5
Presser foot: edge-joining or all-purpose
Needle position: centre

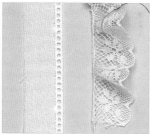

2 Gather the lace following steps 1 to 4 on page 76, creating a firm heading along the gathered edge.

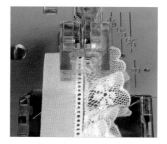

3 With right sides facing, position the pieces under the presser foot, placing the trimmed entredeux edge against the lace heading. Hold the threads taught behind the foot.

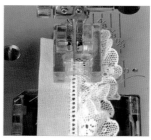

4 Begin to zigzag slowly, ensuring the left needle swing goes into each entredeux hole and the right needle swing just clears the lace heading.

5 Use a pointed tool such as an awl or stiletto to hold the gathers toward the foot. Hold the entredeux taut as you assist the gathered lace to feed evenly.

6 Gently press the stitches with the tip of the iron, taking care not to flatten the gathers of the lace.

7 Sample stitched with matching thread.

ATTACHING ENTREDEUX TO A MITRED LACE CORNER

Corners can easily become distorted with the continual addition of laces to fabric. Attaching entredeux between these elements will help maintain a sharp corner or angle.

Preparation. Attach the lace to the fabric corner following the instructions on page 78. Cut two lengths of entredeux, each approximately 12mm (½") longer than the lace edge at the corner point. Trim the heading from one side of each entredeux piece. Test and adjust the zigzag stitch to suit your entredeux and lace.

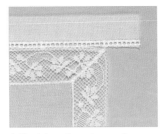

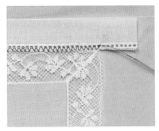

1 Position the trimmed entredeux edge against the lace, the excess extending beyond the corner.

2 Attach the entredeux following the instructions for attaching entredeux to flat lace on page 36.

Suggested machine settings

Zigzag stitch
W: 2.0–2.5
L: 0.75–1.5
Presser foot: basic or edge-joining
Needle position: centre

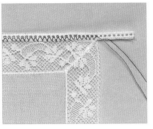

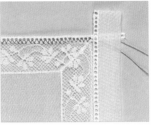

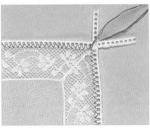

3 At the corner point tie the thread tails in a firm knot. Trim the heading from the remaining side of the entredeux.

5 Position the remaining length of entredeux along the adjacent side, with the excess extending beyond the corner over the previous entredeux.

6 Keeping the thread tails out of the way, zigzag from the corner point. Knot the thread tails. Trim the remaining heading from the entredeux.

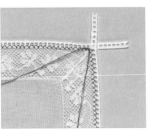

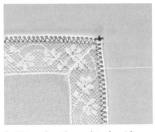

7 **Wrong side.** Pull both sets of thread tails to the wrong side and tie together with a small, firm square knot.

8 Trim the thread tails. Align the two corner holes of the entredeux. Hand-stitch together using very small stitches and fine thread. Trim the entredeux

9 Sample worked using matching sewing thread.

Fabric techniques

From basic hemming and preparation of fabric edges to both decorative and functional appliqué, puffs and tucks, fabric techniques and manipulation plays an important part of all heirloom sewing.

MOCK ROLL HEM

Also French rolled hem

Worked over a tiny fold at the edge of the fabric the stitching of the mock rolled hem will become almost invisible. This hand sewing technique can be used to attach lace and entredeux or just to neaten the edge of a sleeve. The finished width of the hem will be half the width of the fabric folded to the wrong side.

Preparation. Straighten the edge of the fabric following the instructions on page 18.

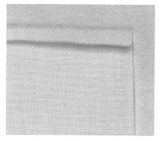

1 Fold a 3mm (⅛") hem to the wrong side of the fabric and press.

2 Take the needle and thread through the folded edge and secure with two or three tiny back stitches.

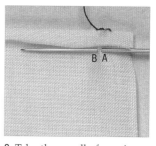

3 Take the needle from A to B just below the raw edge of the hem, picking up a few fabric threads.

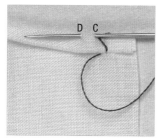

4 Pull the thread through. Take the needle from C to D inside the fabric fold.

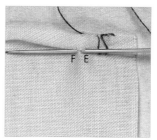

5 Pull the thread through. Take the needle from E to F, picking up a few fabric threads just below the raw edge.

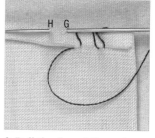

6 Pull the thread through. Take the needle from G to H inside the fabric fold.

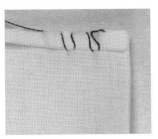

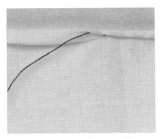

7 Pull the thread through. Groups of parallel lines of stitching are formed along the folded hem.

8 Work four or five stitches in this manner with the last stitch in the fabric fold. Carefully pull the thread until the hem rolls and the stitches disappear inside the fold.

9 Continue working groups of stitches in this manner.

ROLL AND WHIP

By hand *also fine rolled hem*

Rolling and whipping fabric by hand prior to attaching lace or entredeux is considered to be one of the most important techniques in French hand sewing. It requires a little practice and patience but once perfected is worth the time and effort spent.

To ensure an even roll in the fabric, the needle is placed along the edge every so often and the fabric rolled over the needle.

Preparation. Trim any loose or frayed fabric threads along the raw edge before you begin. Knot the end of the thread.

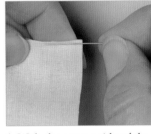

1 With the wrong side of the fabric towards you, hold the top right hand edge between your thumb and fingers. Lay the needle parallel to the edge.

Suggested thread and needle

Thread
fine heirloom sewing cotton

Needle
No. 12 hand appliqué

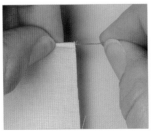

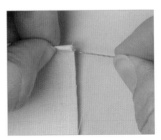

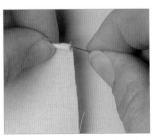

2 Firmly roll the needle and fabric together to the wrong side for one complete turn.

3 Holding the rolled edge firmly, slide the needle from the roll.

4 Slide the needle under the roll and emerge through the upper rolled edge.

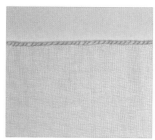

Hint

Roll and whip by hand

To achieve an even smooth roll it is important the needle always emerges through the upper edge of the roll.

5 Pull the thread through. Keeping the thread to the right and angling the needle 45°, slide the needle under the roll and emerging through the upper edge.

6 Pull the thread through. Work a second stitch in the same manner, 2–3mm (¹⁄₁₆"–¹⁄₈") from the first stitch.

7 Continue rolling and whipping in this manner, spacing the stitches evenly. Keep an even tension and pull firmly to create a small, tight roll.

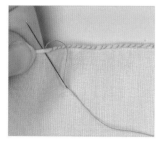

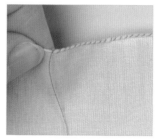

8 Finishing a thread. Take the needle behind the roll and emerge through the upper edge as before, but do not pull through.

9 Wrap the thread firmly around the needle four times in a clockwise direction.

10 While holding the wraps gently, pull the thread through the wraps until it forms a tight knot.

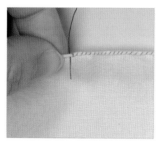

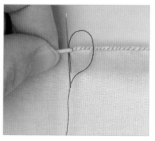

11 Trim the thread close to the knot.

12 Beginning a new thread. Take the needle behind the roll and emerge through the upper edge in the same manner as before, leaving a short tail.

13 Take the needle behind the roll again and re-emerge through the upper edge, but do not pull through.

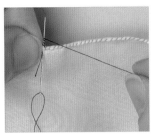

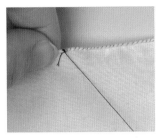

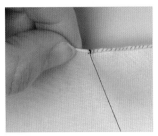

14 Wrap the thread four times around the needle in a clockwise direction.

15 Pull the thread through the wraps as before, forming a firm knot.

16 Trim the thread tail close to the roll. Continue stitching as before.

ROLL AND WHIP

By machine *also fine rolled hem*

The term 'roll and whip' is borrowed from French hand sewing and the technique is successfully imitated by machine. This technique is used to create a neat finish to the raw edge or to add strength before joining lace or entredeux to the fabric. To ensure a fine, even roll the left needle swing should stitch approximately 5mm (³⁄₁₆") onto the fabric and the right needle swing should completely clear the fabric edge.

Preparation. Straighten the fabric edge following the instructions on page 18.

Suggested machine settings

Zigzag stitch

W: 2.75–3.5

L: 0.75–1.0

Presser foot: manual buttonhole

Needle position: left of centre

Hint

Testing machine settings

Different weights of fabric will require different width and length settings. Always make a test sample to determine the best foot to use, the stitch settings and the position of the fabric under the foot.

1 Place the edge of the fabric under the presser foot, slightly to the right of the centre. Hold the machine threads firmly and lower the needle into the fabric.

2 As the needle swings to the right it will clear the fabric edge.

3 Continue stitching along the edge in this manner, causing the fabric edge to roll.

ROLL AND WHIP

Bias and curves

This technique is used to firmly hold any edge that may stretch, such as a neckline, armhole or scalloped hem, prior to adding lace or entredeux. It also works well as a foundation before attaching very narrow binding.

We have marked the stitchline for photographic purpose.

Suggested machine settings

Straight stitch	Zigzag stitch
L: 1.5–2.0	W: 2.0–2.5, L: 0.75–1.0
Presser foot: all-purpose or ¼"	Presser foot: manual buttonhole
Needle position: centre	Needle position: centre

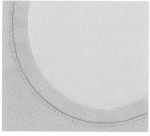

1 Stay stitch within the seam allowance 1.5mm (¹⁄₁₆") from the stitchline, using a short straight stitch.

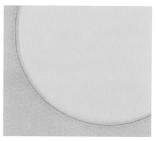

2 Lightly spray starch the edge and press with steam. Trim 1.5mm (¹⁄₁₆") from the stay stitch, leaving a 3mm (⅛") seam allowance.

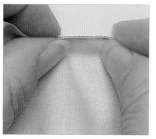

3 Finger press the raw edge to the wrong side rolling the stay stitch to the back.

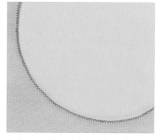

4 From the right side, zigzag a fine rolled hem, encasing the edge and previous stitchline.

ROLL, WHIP AND GATHER

Methods other than the traditional garment construction method of sewing parallel rows of long machine stitches to gather, are used in heirloom sewing for gathering fabric using the basic 'roll and whip' settings.

Encased thread *method one*

This is a quick and very reliable method when gathering long pieces of fabric. Use a quilting thread matching the colour of the fabric. Using this method you can pull the quilting thread and gather from both ends without the worry of breaking the gathering thread.

Suggested machine settings

Zigzag stitch
W: 2.75–3.5, L: 0.75–1.0
Presser foot: manual buttonhole or pintuck
Needle position: just left of centre

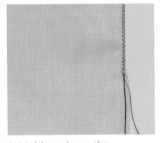

1 Cut the quilting thread longer than the fabric edge and tie a large knot in one end.

2 Holding the quilting thread along the fabric edge, keep the fabric and thread taut with your left hand. Stitch a fine rolled hem, encasing the quilting thread.

3 Pull the quilting thread tails from both ends to gather the fabric.

Gathering stitches *method two*

This method uses a single row of straight gathering stitches encased within a roll and whip hem.
   When gathering long lengths of fabric, pull the gathering from both ends to minimise the strain on the bobbin thread being pulled.

Suggested machine settings

Gathering straight stitch
L: 3.0–3.5
Presser foot: all-purpose
Needle position: centre

Zigzag stitch
W: 2.75–3.5, L: 0.75–1.0
Presser foot: manual buttonhole or pintuck
Needle position: just left of centre

1 Using a strong matching thread, stitch a row of straight stitches 3mm (⅛") from the fabric edge. Leave the thread tails.

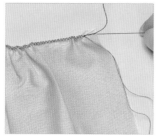

2 Stitch a fine rolled hem, encasing the gathering stitches.

3 Pull the bobbin thread of the gathering stitches to gather the fabric to the required measurement.

CORDED EDGE

This technique is used to neaten and stabilise a shaped edge before attaching lace, entredeux or a decorative hand worked edge.

If you are using gimp or other decorative cord and thread as the feature the piece can be used as is.

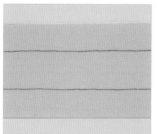

1 Cut the fabric larger than the pattern piece. If using two layers, tack the fabrics together. Lightly spray starch and press with steam.

Suggested machine settings

Zigzag stitch
W: 1.0–1.25, L: 0.75–1.0

Presser foot: single cording or multi-cord

Needle position: centre

Tension: adjust the bobbin tension as for buttonholes

Cord
Gimp cord
No. 8 Perlé cotton

Thread
Cotona no. 80
Tanne no. 80

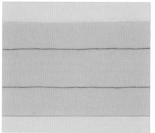

2 Trace the pattern piece onto the fabric, omitting the seam allowance along the edges to be corded.

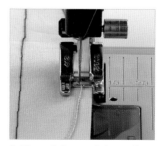

3 Thread the cord through the tunnel in the centre front of the presser foot. Adjusting the width of the stitches to encase the cord, zigzag along the stitchline.

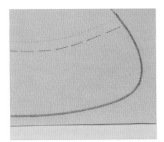 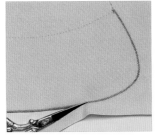 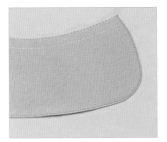

4 Remove the tacking and any visible markings. Lightly spray starch and press from the wrong side to set the stitches.

5 Using fine, sharp scissors, trim the seam allowance close to the zigzag stitches, taking care not to cut the sewing threads.

6 Sample stitched using matching sewing thread and cord.

Hints

Stitching curves

When stitching around a curve, stitch with an even, steady speed, slowly turning the fabric to avoid pivot points. Keep the fabric taut in front of and behind the presser foot.

Scissors

Using a pair of micro-serrated scissors will maintain a grip on fine fabric, especially on the bias grain.

Corded edge

To avoid 'whiskers' along the fabric edge, the zigzag stitch should be very close, but not satin stitch.

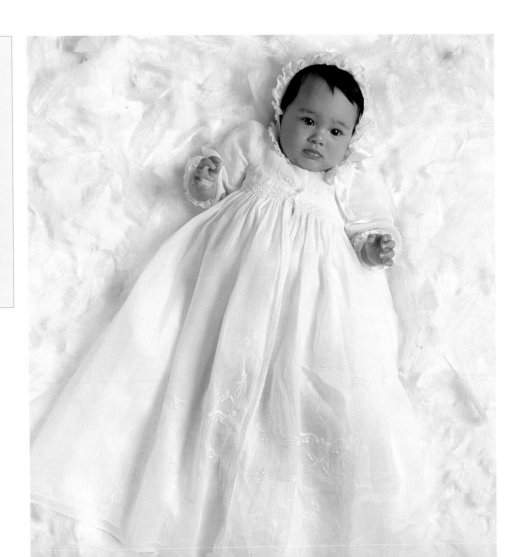

Madeira appliqué

Although found all over the world in both new and antique forms, appliqué worked with the Point de Paris stitch has been produced with such quality and so consistently over the years in the Madeira islands that it is now referred to as Madeira appliqué. For more than 120 years the embroidery from the island of Madeira has been considered among the finest in the world.

The Point de Paris stitch and the techniques of Madeira appliqué create an exciting and decorative addition to tablecloths and other linens, blouses, lingerie and hand made baby and children's clothing.

Fabric made from natural fibres are the most suitable for this type of work. Medium and light weight cotton, linen and silk will give best results.

FOLDED STRAIGHT HEM

Contrary to most other techniques, the side to which the fabric is turned is considered the 'right side'. Only if working with a printed fabric, will the hem need to be turned to the wrong side.

Careful preparation is important to achieve the best results and a straight hem is an excellent start to practise basic preparation and the stitch.

Preparation. Staighten the fabric edge following the instructions on page 18. To mark the fold lines, withdraw one thread at the position for the lower edge and one thread 4mm (³⁄₁₆") from the upper edge of the hem. Lightly spray starch and press the fabric.

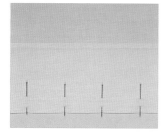

1 Fold and finger press along both pulled threads. Unfold the raw edge. Pin the first fold, placing the pins at right angles.

2 Tack 6mm (¼") from the fold and remove the pins.

3 Smooth the hem and pin the upper edge in place. Tack 6mm (¼") from the pulled thread.

4 Refold the raw edge to the wrong side along the second pulled thread and tack in place.

PIN STITCH

By hand *also Point de Paris*

Suggested thread and needle

Thread
No. 50 mercerized cotton thread is the most appropriate for batiste and fine linen.

Needles
No. 7 crewel needle is a good size to facilitate making small stitches through three layers of fabric.

The stitch, which is variously called Point de Paris, Parisian stitch, pin stitch and Madeira stitch, is one of the loveliest of the decorative stitches. It is a functional stitch, holding two pieces of fabric or fabric and lace together and it forms a series of tiny holes along the stitchline in the fabric surrounding the appliqué. Match the thread colour to the appliqué or hem if possible. The stitches are placed along the folded hem edge, picking up two or three fabric threads along the fold to secure the hem.

Preparation. Prepare the hem using the appropriate method.
Lightly spray starch and press again to ensure a firm base.

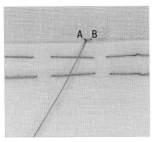

1 Secure the thread and work a small back stitch from A to B in the base fabric, close to the folded edge. Re-emerge at A.

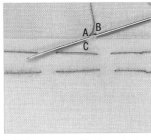

2 Take the needle from B to C, just inside the folded edge. C is directly below A.

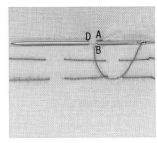

3 Pull the thread through. Take the needle from A to D through the base fabric only.

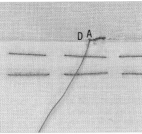

4 Pull the thread through. Work a second stitch from A to D, pulling the thread firmly to open the holes.

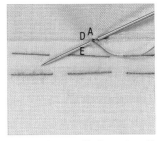

5 Take the needle from A to E just inside the folded edge. E is directly below D.

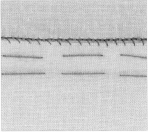

6 Pull the thread through firmly. Continue to repeat steps 3–5 along the folded edge.

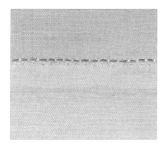

7 Sample worked using matching thread.

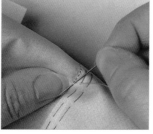

8 **Hand position.** Hold the fabric horizontally with the hem towards you. Work from right to left and keep the fabric taut over your fingers.

Hints

Thread

Test the thread for strength before you begin. Pin stitch puts a lot of stress on the working thread when it is pulled tight to open the holes in the base fabric.

The thread should be no longer than 40cm (15"), as this stitch wears the thread very quickly.

Madeira appliqué

During the 1850's a British subject introduced the techniques of broderie anglaise to the native women of the island of Madeira. Broderie anglaise had recently superseded Ayrshire work and was very popular in Britain. The women of Madeira were already skilful with a needle and showed interest in this new style of white embroidery. They became adept at these stitches and thus a new small industry was born. The popularity of these goods and the quality of the work was such that by the 1880s this style of embroidery became known as broderie Madère, or Madeira work.

PIN STITCH

By machine *also Parisian hemstitch*

This stitch resembles pin stitch by hand. It is used to secure a folded hem or appliqué piece, embroidered medallions or lace in a similar manner. To achieve clear open holes, a needle with a thick shaft is required. Wing needles are specifically designed for this purpose, but a jeans or large universal needle may also be used.

The machine pin stitch is a multi-step stitch, found in the hemstitching menu of most sewing machines. The stitch pattern resembles the letter 'L', or a reversed 'L', repeating the forward and reverse stitches and, on some machines, the sideways stitches. The appearance of the stitch may vary slightly between sewing machine brands. Refer to your machine manual and test your stitch settings before you begin. We used a slightly larger stitch for photographic purposes.

Preparation. Prepare the hem using the appropriate method. Lightly spray starch and press again to ensure a firm base.

Suggested threads and needle

Thread
No. 80, 100 or 110 mercerized sewing machine cotton

Needles
No. 100 wing
No. 100 or 110 jeans
No.110 or 120 all-purpose needle

Suggested machine settings

Zigzag stitch
W: 1.5–2.0, L: 2.0

Presser Foot: open-toed embroidery foot

Needle position: centre

Tension: bobbin tightened or top tension loosened

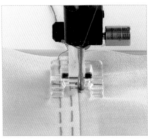

1 Place the fabric under the presser foot, ensuring the forward and reverse stitches are stitched along the edge of the folded hem through the base fabric only.

2 The left needle swing enters the fabric fold, catching a few fabric threads.

Hint

Feed tension

Allow the feed dogs to move backwards and forwards freely to feed the fabric under the presser foot without tension.

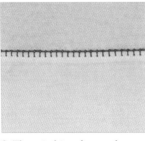
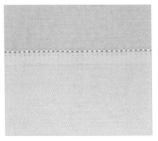

3 The stitching forms clear holes along the edge of the folded hem.

4 Machine pin stitch worked using matching sewing thread.

SCALLOPED APPLIQUÉ HEM

The scalloped appliqué hem is a delicate decorative finish not only for baby garments but also lingerie, collars, sleeve and bodice trims.

Preparation. Determine the size of the scallops and make a template following the instructions on page 19. Neaten the fabric edge along a pulled thread to ensure you are working on the straight grain. Press and lightly spray starch the fabrics.

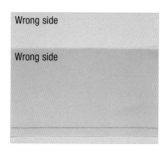

1 With the right side of the appliqué piece facing the wrong side of the garment, pin, tack and stitch along the lower edge.

2 Press to set the stitches. Grade the seam allowance to 4mm (³⁄₁₆") leaving the widest grade on the appliqué piece.

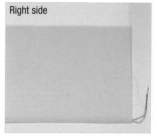

3 Press the seam firmly towards the garment piece. From the right side, understitch close to the seam.

4 Finger press a foldline on the appliqué hem and fold to the right side of the garment piece.

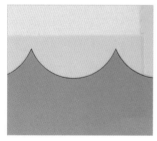

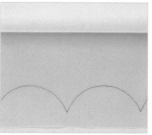

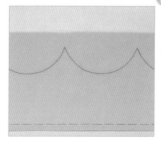

5 Aligning the straight edge of the template with the folded edge, place the template over the appliqué hem. Lightly mark the scallop foldline with a pencil or chalk pencil.

6 Unfold the fabrics. Stay stitch on the scallop foldline using a very fine thread and a short stitch length. Press to set the stitches.

7 Refold the fabrics with the appliqué hem uppermost. Ensuring the appliqué hem is smooth, tack the hem 6mm (¼") from the folded edge.

Hint

Pin stitch holes

If the holes are not clear and open, refer to your machine manual to fine-tune the stitch.

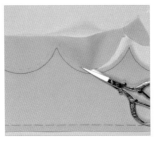 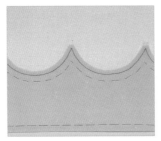 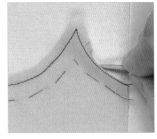

8 Measure and mark the cutting line 4mm (³⁄₁₆") above the stay stitchline. Using small sharp scissors, carefully trim along the cutting line, taking care not to cut the base fabric.

9 Ensuring the appliqué hem is smooth, pin the scalloped edge in place. Tack 6mm (¼") inside the stay stitchline. Remove the pins.

10 Working a small section at a time, carefully clip the curve of the first scallop. Fold the raw edge under, placing the stay stitching on the fold. Use a moistened toothpick to help grip the seam allowance.

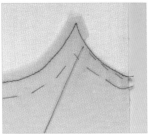 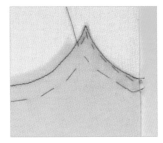 

11 Tack close to the folded edge.

12 At the peaks, fold the tip of the fabric first, then the sides to avoid any puckering. Tack in place.

13 Pinstitch the scallops by hand or machine. Remove the tacking.

Hints

Staystitch The stay stitchline makes turning back the scallops easier and reinforces the points.

Machine stitching When machine stitching on a single layer of fabric hold the fabric taut in front of and behind the presser foot, preventing the fabric from puckering.

Turning peaks It is important to fold the seam allowances at the peaks carefully to avoid puckering. When nearing the peak, fold the seam allowance at the tip to the wrong side, before folding the seam allowances along each side.

Puffing

A puffing band is a strip of fine fabric, gathered on both sides and inserted into a seam. It can add a delicate touch to heirloom garments and other projects. The length of the fabric strip to be gathered should measure two to three times the finished length. The more gathers you create, the more difficult it will be to attach neatly because of the amount of bulk in the seam allowance. Too few gathers may not create the desired effect. To test, experiment with different fabric weights and ratios before you begin.

PUFFING

Using a sewing machine

This method of making a puffing band or strip is relatively quick and easy, perfect when puffing long lengths of fabric.

Preparation. Measure and cut the fabric strip 12mm (½") wider and two to three times longer than the finished measurement. Mark the halfway and quarter points with a chalk pencil or water-soluble marker.

1 Cut a length of quilting thread longer than the fabric and matching the fabric colour. Place a very large knot in the end of the quilting thread.

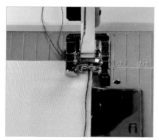

2 Place the quilting thread under the presser foot, 2mm (⅟₁₆") from the raw edge of the fabric.

3 Stitch, using a fine zigzag that clears the fabric edge on the right, encasing the quilting thread. Take care not to stitch into the quilting thread.

4 The zigzag stitch will roll the raw edge of the fabric over the quilting thread enclosing it in the roll.

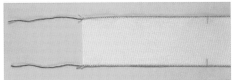

5 Repeat on the remaining long edge of the fabric strip.

6 Pull the unknotted end of the quilting threads evenly along both sides to gather one half of the strip.

7 Repeat for the opposite end to gather the remaining half. Gently adjust the gathers until the strip is the required length.

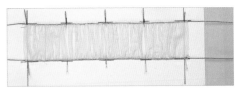

8 Pin to a blocking board and manipulate the pleats so they are straight and even. Lightly spray starch and steam well, holding the iron just above the fabric. Leave to dry on the board.

9 Puffing strip prepared using matching thread, ready to be inserted into a seam or trimmed with entredeux, piping or lace.

PUFFING

Using a smocking pleater

This method of gathering fabric will cause small pleats along the stitchline unless a smocking staystitch is worked along the innermost holding rows. We used stem stitch following the instructions on page 58.

Preparation. Measure and cut the fabric strip 3cm (1¼") wider and two to three times longer than the finished measurements. Lightly spray starch the fabric and press well before pleating. This helps the fabric slide off the needles and gives body to the puffed fabric.

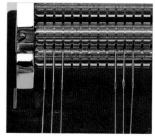

1 Thread three half space needles to fit along each side of the fabric strip.

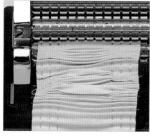

2 Roll the fabic onto a pleating rod. Align the edges 5mm (³⁄₁₆") past the outermost needles. Pleat the fabric, ensuring it is caught evenly.

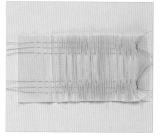

3 Remove the threads from the seam allowance at each end. Tie off the threads at one end, leaving them long and uncut at the opposite end.

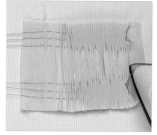

4 Pull up the pleats so they sit close together. Press the seam allowances only.

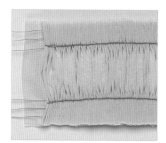

5 Using one strand of matching thread, smock a row of stem stitch just outside each innermost holding row, pulling each stitch tight.

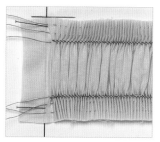

6 Gently work the pleats apart until the strip is the required length. Pin to a blocking board and manipulate the smocking so the puffing is straight and even.

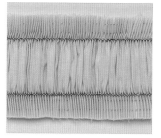

7 Lightly spray starch and steam, holding the iron above the fabric. Leave to dry before removing from the board.

PUFFING MEDALLION

Puffed medallions are used for round pillows, neck rolls and bonnets or inserted into garments. This type of puffing is prepared using a template with a drawn circle.

Preparation. Cut the fabric strip 12mm (½") wider than the finished width required and double the length of the outer measurement of the circle. Mark the quarter points on both long edges.

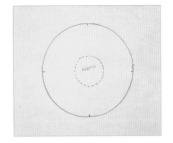

1 Draw the circle template onto heavy paper and mark the quarter points.

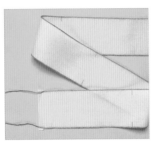

2 Leaving a 1cm (⅜") seam allowance at each end, prepare both long sides following steps 2–5 on pages 53–54.

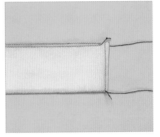

3 Stitch the short ends together to form a circle, using a fine French seam. Ensure the quilting threads are not caught in the seam.

4 Matching the quarter marks, pin one edge of the fabric to the outer marked circle on the template.

5 Draw up the gathering thread from each end and further pin the fabric around the circle.

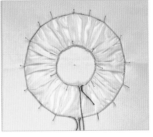

6 Draw up the inner edge of the fabric to fit the inner circle on the template. Pin in place around the inner edge, adjusting the gathers so they are straight and evenly spaced.

7 Lightly spray starch the puffing and steam well, holding the iron just above the fabric. Leave to dry before removing from the board.

PUFFING WITH ENTREDEUX

Entredeux attached to puffing will camouflage the seam and stabilise the gathered fabric. Be mindful that it is easiest to apply when the puffing is not too dense and the fabric is very lightweight.

Preparation. Gather the fabric using your chosen method. Cut two lengths of entredeux to the required measurement.

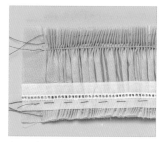

1 With right sides together, place one length of entredeux over the puffing strip, aligning the ditch of the entredeux with the innermost holding row. Tack in place.

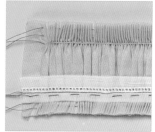

2 Stitch in the ditch, just inside the smocking stitches. Remove the innermost holding row only.

Suggested stitch settings
Neatening the seam on the wrong side;

Zigzag stitch
W: 4.0, L: 1.0

Stitching seam on the right side;

Zigzag stitch
W: 1.5, L: 1.0

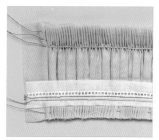

3 Stitch again, 2mm (1/16") from the first stitching line.

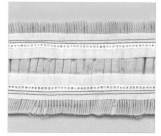

4 Repeat for the remaining side, ensuring the gathers in the puffing remain straight and even.

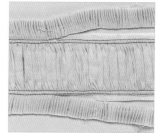

5 **Wrong side.** Trim the gathered seam allowance only, close to the second line of stitching on both sides.

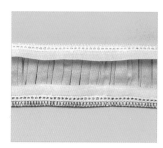

6 Roll and whip the entredeux heading over the raw edges, using a close zigzag stitch, wide enough to clear the edge of the fabric on the right and cover the stitching on the left.

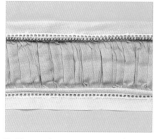

7 Press the seam away from the entredeux, towards the fabric.

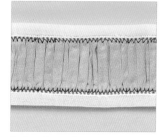

8 On the right side, zigzag over the seam. The right needle swing catching the fabric and the left needle swing entering the holes of the entredeux.

STEM STITCH ON SMOCKING

When a puffing strip is gathered using a smocking pleater it is necessary to work a row of smocking staystitch along the innermost holding row to secure the gathers. After working only a few stitches the row will appear to slope. It is not crooked, the fabric is skewing. Keep stitching and the row will appear straight.

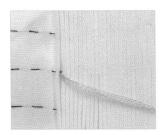

1 Secure the thread on the back of the fabric. Bring it to the front between the first and second pleats.

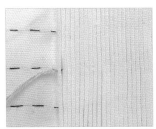

2 Take the needle from right to left through the first pleat.

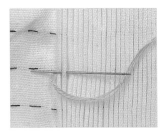

3 Pull the thread through. With the thread below the needle and the needle held horizontally, take it from right to left through the second pleat.

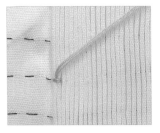

4 Pull the thread through until the stitch sits snugly against the pleat.

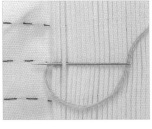

5 Keeping the thread below the needle, take the needle from right to left through the third pleat.

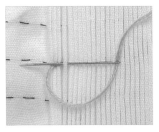

6 Pull the thread through as before. Keeping the thread below the needle, take the needle from right to left through the fourth pleat.

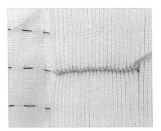

7 Continue to the end of the row in the same manner.

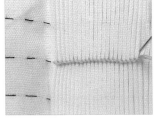

8 To end off, take the needle to the back of the fabric through the valley behind the last stem stitch.

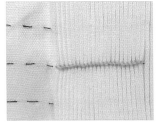

9 Pull the thread through and secure it on the back of the fabric. Completed line of stem stitch.

Tucks

Tucks create a wonderful opportunity to add texture and interest to a project. They are versatile and combine beautifully with other heirloom techniques. Pintucks can be used as an embellishment for baby gowns, lingerie, adult blouses, nightgowns, underwear such as petticoats and cushions.

Tucks can also be used to create a practical and decorative hemline, see page 118.

Tucks fall into two basic categories.

Basic tucks, include pintucks, blind tucks, shell edge tucks, whipped pintucks and release tucks.

Twin needle tucks, include corded twin needle tucks, scalloped or shaped tucks and cross-over tucks.

Regardless of the type of tuck you wish to include, additional fabric must be added. Increase the finished measurement to allow for each tuck by adding twice the tuck size.

For example, each 1cm (⅜") finished tuck requires 2cm (¾") additional fabric.

MARKING TUCKS

Pin and press

This method is used to mark deeper tucks and for tucks around hemlines. It is the most versatile method when working with fine fabrics. If you are working multiple tucks, it is advisable to pin, press and stitch one tuck at a time for the best result. Use a measuring gauge when marking the foldline for each tuck.

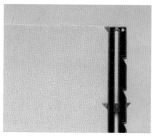

1 With the right side facing, measure from the raw edge to determine the position for the fold of the first tuck. Set the measuing guage to this measurement.

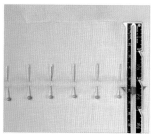

2 Using this measurement, work along the fabric edge, placing pins approximately 2cm (¾") apart.

Hints

Stitching tucks

Tucks should always be worked with the stitching from the top thread on the right side of the tuck.

Long tucks

When preparing tucks on long pieces of fabric or around a hem, pin and press a small section at a time.

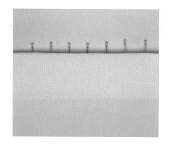

3 Gently lift the fabric and fold, making sure the pins extend from the foldline.

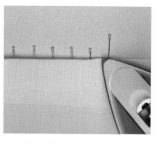

4 Using the tip of the iron, press the foldline, gently pushing each pin out of the way as you reach it. Continue pressing until all pins have been removed.

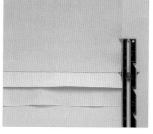

5 **Multiple tucks.** Stitch the first tuck. Re-determine the measurement for the foldline for any subsequent tucks, measuring from the previous tuck stitchline. Repeat steps 2–4.

MARKING TUCKS

Drawn thread

This works well when making multiple or very long, narrow tucks on fine fabric. This method is not suitable for linen where the slubs can cause gaps on the foldline.

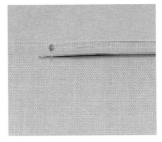

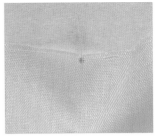

1 Using a needle or pin, ease a thread from the edge of the fabric at the position of the foldline for the tuck.

2 Gently begin to draw the thread out of the fabric.

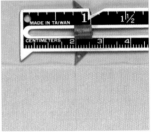

3 If the thread breaks, find the break and use the needle to ease the thread out at the break point.

4 Continue drawing the thread out until reaching the opposite side.

5 Multiple tucks. Use a measuring gauge to determine the placement for the remaining tucks.

Hints

Tucks

It is important that tucks are worked perfectly even. Poorly worked tucks will detract from an otherwise well constructed garment.

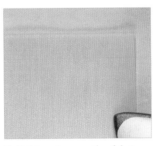

6 Following steps 1–4, remove the threads at the marked positions for any remaining pintucks.

7 Fold and press the fabric along a pulled thread.

MARKING TUCKS

Water-soluble fabric marker

This method is most suitable for larger tucks and is usually only used as a last resort. The fabric must be washed before the tucks can be pressed as heat can make the marks permanent. Finger press the foldlines and always stitch all the tucks before rinsing and pressing the piece.

1 Rule the foldline following a fabric thread on the right side of the fabric.

2 **Multiple tucks.** Measure and mark the parallel foldlines for the required number of tucks.

3 Fold and finger press the fabric along a marked line.

BASIC TUCK

By machine

These tucks are stitched along a fabric fold. The width of the tucks may vary from very narrow 2mm (¹⁄₁₆") wide pintucks to 2.5cm (1") or wider. Test the size and spacing of the tucks before commencing a project. Prepare the fabric by lightly misting with water or spray starch and pressing. Always fold, press and stitch one tuck at a time for the best result.

Gauging the width.

The width of the tucks can be gauged using one of the following methods.
1 Choose a presser foot and needle position suitable for the required tuck width.
2 Align the folded edge with one of the lines on the base plate, if they match the desired width of the tuck.
3 Place a piece of tape on the base plate beside the presser foot marking the width of the tuck.

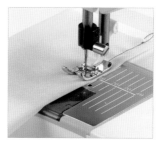

1 Place the fold of the fabric under the presser foot, so the needle is positioned the required distance from the folded edge. Using a short stitch length, sew the tuck, holding the fabric taut in front of and behind the presser foot.

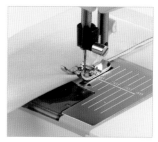

1 **Pintucks** are stitched in a similar manner to basic tucks, placing the stitchline very close to the folded edge.

CORDED TUCK

To achieve texture, cord can be added inside the tuck. This method is also used to add weight at the hemline of fine fabric or make a ruched panel for drawing up a baby bonnet, or sleeve cuff-line.

Suitable cord. Choose a cord suitable for the size of the tuck and the weight of the fabric. Cordonnet, no. 8 perlé cotton, no. 10 or no. 20 crochet cotton or soft cotton are all suitable.

1 Mark and prepare the tuck using your chosen method. On the wrong side, place a thin cord into the foldline of the tuck.

2 Place the fabric under the presser foot, ensuring the cord is positioned in the channel of the foot and the needle positioned close to the cord.

Hint

Corded tuck

Experiment with various weights and colours of cord for a more pronounced or decorative tuck.

3 Stitch, taking care not to catch the cord in the machine stitches. Use your fingernail to push against the cord and keep it even in the fabric fold.

4 Multiple corded tucks stitched with matching thread.

PINTUCK

By hand

In French hand sewing, the fabric thread is removed in one length to mark the foldline and is then used to handstitch the tuck, making the stitching invisible.

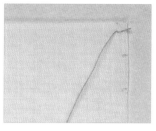

1 Bring the thread to the front through the fabric fold at one end and secure within the seam allowance.

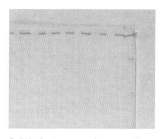

2 Work tiny evenly spaced running stitches the required distance from the folded edge.

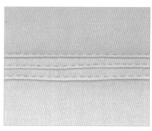

3 Work the remaining pintucks in the same manner.

RELEASE TUCK

Release tucks are stitched in a similar way to other tucks, but are finished part way to create fullness.

They are often used from the shoulder of a ladies blouse or nightgown to add fullness for the bust, around the top of a skirt instead of gathers or on an A-line baby daygown or child's nightgown. Release tucks can be any width and, although usually made with a single needle, can be made with a twin needle for a less full, decorative effect.

The thread tails will need to be pulled to the back and tied off at the tuck ends to make the release point inconspicuous.

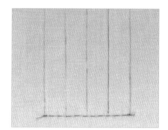

1 Mark the foldline for the tucks using your chosen method. Tack to mark the release point or depth of the tuck.

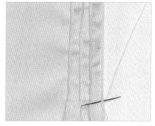

2 Fold and stitch the required number of tucks, stitching from the release point to the edge. Take the top and bobbin threads separately to the wrong side.

3 **Wrong side**. Tie each pair of top and bobbin threads together snugly against the fabric. Trim, leaving short tails.

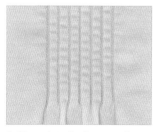

4 Completed release tucks.

RELEASE TUCK

Reverse threaded

Stitching reverse threaded tucks works well for very narrow release tucks, and is even more impressive on wider tucks.

Preparation. Remove the top thread from the machine and pull up a length of the bobbin thread.

1 Using a needle threader, thread the needle from the back to the front with the bobbin thread.

2 Continue threading the machine in reverse. The end of the bobbin thread should now be located at the top of the sewing machine where the spool of thread would be positioned.

3 Place the folded fabric under the presser foot at the release point. Lower the needle. The thread wraps the folded edge.

4 Gently pull the top thread to tighten any looseness caused when lowering the needle. Hold the top thread firm as you make the first few stitches.

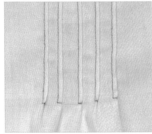

5 Completed reverse threaded tucks.

SHELL TUCKS

These decorative tucks are formed by sewing over a fabric fold, allowing the needle to swing clear of the folded edge. The most suitable fabrics are soft, lightweight woven cotton or cotton blend. Shell tucks are often used as a decorative multi-tuck on lingerie, nightwear and delicate baby and children's clothing. A single shell edge tuck makes a lovely finishing detail around the neckline and armholes of lingerie or baby wear.

Shell edge tucks can also be used to make scalloped piping by stitching along the edge of a folded bias strip.

Preparation. Test your settings first to determine the size of the scallops you wish to achieve. The right needle swing should clear the fabric fold, causing the fabric to pucker and form a scalloped edge.

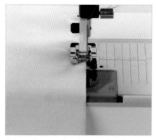

1 Position the folded fabric under the presser foot so the right needle swing clears the folded edge.

2 Stitch along the folded edge, ensuring the right needle swing clears and puckers the edge for each stitch.

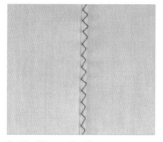

3 **Shallow shell tucks** created with zigzag stitch.

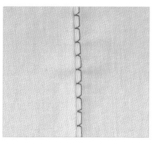

4 **Medium shell tucks** created with blind hemstitch.

5 **Deep shell tucks** stitched on the bias with blind hemstitch.

6 Parallel rows of **deep shell tucks** stitched on the bias using matching thread.

7 **Scallop piping.** A shell edge can be stitched on a bias strip and used in place of piping.

WHIPPED TUCK

Whipped tucks are made using a very small zigzag stitch. They are often used as decorative tucks on lingerie, nightwear and delicate baby and children's clothing. Whipped tucks can also be used to make tucked panels for insertion into a garment. The thread can be fine and the same colour as the fabric so as to blend when pressed, or contrasting colour and thickness to create texture and highlight.

Preparation. Mark and prepare the tucks using your chosen method. Test your machine settings before you begin. The left needle swing should enter the fabric two to three threads from the folded edge and the right needle swing just clear the folded edge.

Suggested machine settings

Zigzag stitch

W: 0.75–1.0

L: 1.0–1.5

Tension: reduce top tension slightly to avoid puckering

Presser foot: all-purpose or edge-joining

Needle position: centre

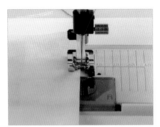

1 Position the folded fabric under the presser foot, ensuring the right needle swing clears the edge.

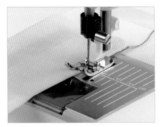

2 Stitch with a small zigzag stitch, enclosing the folded edge.

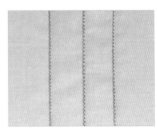

3 Completed whipped tuck.

TWIN NEEDLE TUCKS

Twin needle tucks are created using a twin needle and a special grooved foot, which complements the needle size. Thread your sewing machine for the twin needles following your machine manual. The two top threads work with the bobbin thread, which forms a small zigzag on the wrong side of the work, pulling the two rows of top threads together to form the tuck. The smaller the stitch length, the more likely the tucks will sit up and form a ridge. Test your tucks to ensure correct balance of thread, needle, foot and spacing.

Preparation. Mark the first tuck using your chosen method. The remaining tucks are spaced using the ridges under the presser foot as a guide. Alternatively mark all the tucks.

Fabric	Twin needle	Presser foot
Very fine eg: Swiss voile, batiste, cotton lawn	No. 1.6/70	9-groove pintuck foot
Medium weight eg: cotton sateen, dress-weight batiste, fine linen	No. 2.0/75	5 or 7-groove foot
Heavier weight eg: tightly woven cotton or medium linen	No. 2.5/80	3 or 5-groove foot

1 Holding the threads at the beginning to engage the bobbin thread, stitch along the marked line.

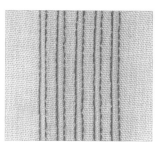

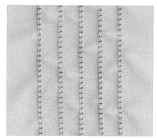

2 Stitch the next tuck, aligning the first tuck in a groove under the presser foot. Alternatively, follow a marked line.

3 Multiple twin needle tucks.

4 **Wrong side.** To secure the thread tails, take to the back separately at the end of the tuck. Tie the top and bobbin threads together snugly against the fabric. Trim leaving short tails.

TWIN NEEDLE TUCKS

Corded

These types of tucks are only suitable where both ends of the tuck can be secured in a seam. Different sewing machines have different methods for incorporating the cord under the fabric. Some have a special base plate with a hole and guide directly in front of the needles through which the cord is threaded. Follow the instructions in your machine manual. Alternatively place the cord over the base plate, passing it between the two needles. Thread the machine in the same manner as for twin needle tucks.

Preparation. Mark the position for the tuck using your chosen method. Secure the end of the cord on the wrong side at the beginning of the tuck line.

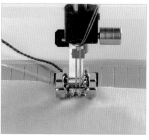

1 Position the fabric under the presser foot, holding the cord straight. Lower the needles, ensuring the cord is centred between them.

2 Straight stitch along the cord.

3 Press the tucks first from the wrong side on a well padded surface to prevent flattening the tucks.

TWIN NEEDLE TUCK

Scalloped

Twin needle tucks can be shaped with gentle curves or geometric peaks. It is important to plan and mark the fabric for shaped tucks.

Preparation. Make a template following the instructions on page 19.

Straighten the fabric edge, lightly mist with water or spray starch and press.

Refer to the fabric, needle and presser foot guide on page 66.

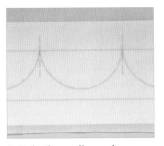

1 Rule the scallop reference line and pivot lines onto the fabric with a chalk pencil. Position the template, aligning the line and points. Trace in the scallops.

2 Begin stitching, aligning the marked scalloped line with the centre of the foot.

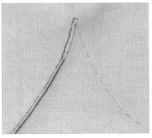

3 Stop at the pivot point with the needles in the down position.

4 Lift the presser foot and gently pivot the fabric, placing the presser foot across the top of the pivot point. Turn the fly wheel by hand and make a stitch across the top of the point. The right needle stitches into the same position.

Hint

Fabric markers

When using a water-soluble fabric marker, always remove all marks before pressing the fabric, as heat will set the marks and make them permanent.

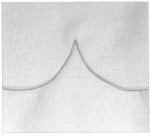

5 Lift the presser foot again and gently pivot the fabric, placing the presser foot in the direction of the next scallop.

6 Completed twin needle scalloped tuck.

PRESSING TUCKS

To achieve crisp tucks it is important to press carefully at each stage using spray starch and steam.

1 Stitch the required number of tucks. Press each tuck while folded, to set the stitches along each tuck. Lay the fabric flat and finger-press the tucks in the desired direction.

2 Wrong side. Steam press, pushing the side of the iron firmly against the stitchline of each tuck. Take care that no pleats are formed between the tucks.

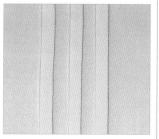

3 Turn to the right side and press again.

STRAIGHTENING TUCKS

When stitching several parallel tucks, the fabric will appear out of shape with the tucks looking distorted or on the bias. This is more obvious when working on a large piece of fabric.

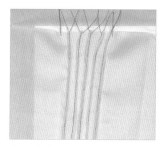

1 Lightly mist the tucked fabric with water or spray starch. Pin one end onto an ironing or blocking board.

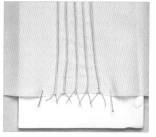

2 Gently pull the other end, straightening the tucks. Hold the fabric taut and pin to the board. The pins should slant to the outside to prevent the fabric sliding on the pin.

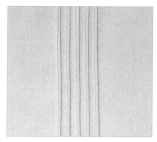

3 Press the tucks and leave the fabric to dry before removing.

Lace techniques

The extensive use of lace is an important component in heirloom sewing. Many different types of lace are used for trims and edgings or several lengths can be joined to create a fine lace fabric.

ATTACHING LACE TO FABRIC

Rolled seam *method one*

This method is very quick and best used for decorative purposes, or where there will be minimal strain on the join.

Preparation. Straighten the edge of the fabric following the instructions on page 18. Mist the fabric and the lace with water and press with steam. Test and adjust the zigzag width so it clears the edge of the fabric on the right and catches the lace heading on the left.

1 With right sides together, position the lace 3mm (⅛") from the edge of the fabric and tack. Align the right hand side of the lace heading with the centre of the presser foot.

2 Holding the fabric and lace taut, stitch along the centre of the lace heading with a short straight stitch.

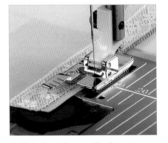

3 Stitch a fine rolled seam, encasing the lace heading and fabric edge. Adjust the zigzag width so it clears the edge of the fabric on the right and just catches the lace heading on the left.

4 Roll the seam away from the lace between your fingers

5 Using the side of the iron, press the rolled seam away from the lace.

6 **Right side**. Tiny stitches will be visible along the seam on the right side.

7 Wrong side of sample stitched using matching sewing threads.

Rolled seam *method two*

This method is used when extra strength is required or when you want to avoid visible stitches on the front of your work.

The best result is achieved when this technique is worked on the straight grain of the fabric.

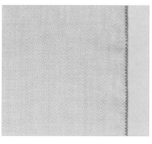

1 Roll and whip the straight edge of the fabric following the instructions on page 42.

2 With right sides together position the lace over the fabric, placing the lace heading alongside the rolled edge.

Suggested machine settings

Zigzag Stitch:
W: 2.75–3.5
L: 0.75–1.0
Presser foot: manual buttonhole or pintuck
Needle position: centre

3 Stitch a fine rolled seam, encasing the previous rolled hem and the lace heading.

4 Using the side of the iron, press the seam away from the lace.

5 Sample stitched using matching sewing thread.

Suggested machine settings

Straight stitch
L: 2.0
Presser foot: all purpose or ¼"

Zigzag stitch
W: 1.0–1.5, L: 0.75–1.0
Presser foot: all purpose or manual buttonhole

Rolled seam method three

This is the most accurate and secure method for attaching lace. It is particularly useful for attaching lace to a curved or shaped edge.

Preparation. Straighten the fabric edge following the instructions on page 18. Gently pull the gimp thread without gathering the lace.

1 With the right sides facing, position the lace over the fabric, leaving no less than a 1cm (⅜") seam allowance. Tack in place just inside the heading.

2 Stitch along the centre of the lace heading using a small straight stitch.

3 Remove the tacking. Turn to the wrong side and press the seam allowance away from the lace, using the side of the iron.

4 Working from the right side, secure the lace with a tiny zigzag stitch, adjusting the width so it covers the lace heading. Press to set the stitches.

5 **Wrong side.** Trim the seam allowance close to the zigzag. Hold the scissors flat with the fabric being cut resting over the tips of your fingers.

ATTACHING LACE TO FABRIC

Pin stitch

This is a decorative finish used when securing lace edging or insertion. The machine technique imitates the French hand sewing technique of Point de Paris, see page 48.

Preparation. Straighten the fabric edge, following the instructions on page 18. Lightly spray starch and press. Test and adjust your machine settings to suit your lace before you begin, ensuring the width of the stitches encase the lace heading.

Suggested machine settings

Straight stitch
L: max 2.0
Presser foot: all-purpose or ¼"
Needle position: centre

Pin stitch
W: 2.0–4.0, L: 1.0–1.5
Presser foot: embroidery or open-toe
Needle: no.110 jeans
Needle position: centre

1 With right sides facing, position the lace over the fabric, leaving no less than a 1cm (⅜") seam allowance. Tack in place just below the lace heading.

2 Stitch along the centre of the lace heading, using a small straight stitch.

3 Remove the tacking. Turn to the wrong side and press the seam allowance away from the lace, using the side of the iron.

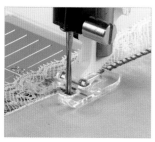

4 Change the needle and presser foot. With the right side facing, pin stitch along the edge, ensuring the stitches encase the lace heading.

5 Wrong side. Trim the seam allowance close to the pin stitch. Hold the scissors flat with the fabric being cut resting over the tips of your fingers.

6 Machine pin stitch worked using matching thread.

ATTACHING LACE TO SCALLOPED EDGE

Suggested machine settings

Straight stitch

L: 1.5–2.0

Presser foot: all-purpose or ¼"

Needle position: centre

Zigzag stitch

W: 1.5–2.0, L: 0.75–1.0

Presser foot: manual buttonhole or pintuck

Needle position: centre

Applying lace using the following method allows you to shape the lace on a flat surface, avoiding distorting the curve. Narrow lace will result in smoother curves.

Preparation. Determine the number and size of scallops required and prepare a template following the instructions on page 19. Lightly spray starch and press the fabric. Mist the lace with water. Press with steam to shrink the lace. Rule or tack the scallop reference line and pivot lines onto the fabric. Use a lace shaping board when positioning and shaping the lace.

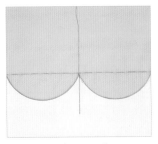

1 Position the template below the scallop reference line and trace the scallops. Alternatively, align the template base with the raw edge and trace.

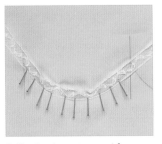

2 Beginning at one side seam, leave a 2.5cm (1") tail. Pin the lower edge of the lace to the traced line, angling the pins over the lace heading and placing them 1cm (⅜") apart.

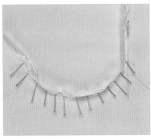

3 Pin to the pivot line of the first scallop, taking care not to stretch the lace. Insert a pin on the pivot line above the pivot point.

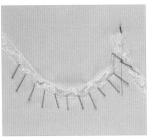

4 Forming a pleat, turn the lace and position the heading along the next scallop. Lightly mark the headings at the pivot point.

5 Continue pinning the lace along the next scallop. Ease out and gently pull the gimp thread at the upper edge of the lace at regular intervals until the lace lies flat.

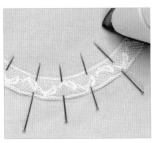

6 Smooth out the lace with your fingernail and press with the tip of the iron. Free this section from the board, reposition the pins through the lace and fabric only.

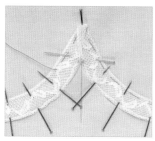

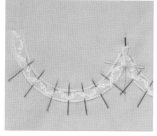

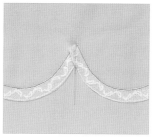

7 Tack the lace to the fabric just below the heading of the upper lace edge, keeping the pleat free.

8 Continue until reaching the starting point and trim the lace leaving a 2.5cm (1") tail.

9 Stitch along the upper lace heading with a short straight stitch, keeping the pleat free. Remove the tacking. Gently press the seam to set the stitches.

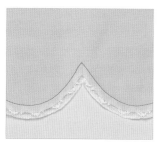

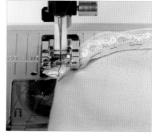

10 With the wrong side uppermost, trim the fabric away from behind the lace, leaving a 6mm (¼") seam allowance.

11 Clip into the pivot points and around the curves at 1cm (⅜") intervals. Press the seam allowance away from the lace and tack to secure.

12 Pushing the lace pleat to the wrong side, fold with right sides together. Stitch the pleat from the pivot point to the marked point. Pivot and stitch back to the starting point.

13 Stitch a small zigzag enclosing the previous stitchlines. Press to set the stitches and trim close to the zigzag. Press the seam to one side.

14 Working from the right side, secure the lace with a tiny zigzag stitch that covers the lace heading. Gently press to set the stitches.

Hint

Shaping lace

Use a pin to pick up the top gimp thread in the lace heading. Gently pull to gather and shape the lace to fit the curve.

ATTACHING GATHERED LACE TO FABRIC

Suggested machine settings

Zigzag Stitch:
W: 2.75–3.5, L: 0.75–1.0
Presser foot: manual buttonhole
Needle position: just left of centre

Lace is easily gathered by pulling the threads in the heading. It is always a good idea to gather from both ends toward the centre wherever possible, especially on long lengths of lace. The gimp thread at the upper edge of the lace is usually the strongest and is pulled first.

1 Mark the centre and quarter marks of the fabric and lace with coloured thread.

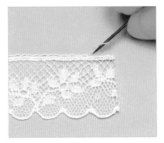

2 Ease out the end of the gimp thread at the upper edge of the lace heading.

3 Pull taut, gathering the lace to approximately the length required. Distribute the gathers evenly.

Hint

Gathering lace

Pulling several threads of the lace heading is a little more time consuming than pulling a single thread, however it sets the gathers more firmly and creates a firm ribbon of threads that will lay very flat on the fabric. Take care not to distort the lace when arranging the gathers.

Be mindful of the fullness of the gathers. Too many gathers are not necessarily better, as they tend to obscure the pattern in the lace. Too few gathers can give the appearance that you did not have sufficient lace. A ratio of approximately 2:1 lace to fabric usually works well.

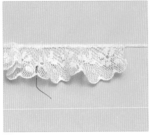

4 Carefully pull all remaining threads in the lace heading, one at a time.

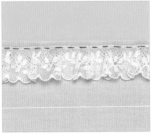

5 With right sides together and matching marks, place the edge of the gathered lace 3mm (⅛") from the raw edge. Tack in place. Remove the thread marks.

6 Adjust the zigzag width so it clears the edge of the fabric on the right and just catches the lace heading on the left.

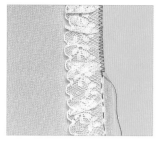

7 Stitch the lace in place with a rolled seam.

8 Press the seam away from the lace. Sample stitched using matching thread.

MITRING A LACE CORNER

Mitring a lace corner prior to attaching the lace ensures that the corner is precise. The lace edge or insertion is then stitched to the fabric in one movement.

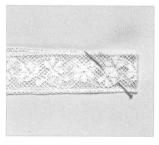

1 With right sides together, fold the lace and mark a 45° angle.

2 Stitch from the widest point to the folded edge just below the heading, using a short straight stitch. Taking care not to stitch into the heading, stop with the needle in the down position.

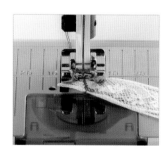

3 Lift the presser foot and pivot the lace. Pull the thread tails back under the presser foot over the original row of straight stitches.

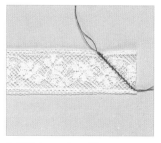

4 Stitch again with a narrow zigzag stitch covering the previous stitchline and thread tails. Press to set the stitches.

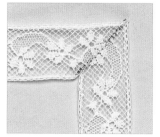

5 Trim carefully close to the zigzag stitches. Do not cut into the lace heading at the pivot point. Lightly spray starch and press.

6 Position the lace on the fabric corner leaving a 1cm (⅜") seam allowance behind the lace and tack.

7 Straight stitch along the lace heading pivoting at the mitred corner. Press to set the stitches. Mist with water and press again. Remove the tacking.

8 On the wrong side, clip each seam allowance to the corner point.

9 Press the seam allowance away from the lace.

10 On the right side, secure the lace with a narrow zigzag stitch, pivoting at the corners.

11 On the wrong side, trim the seam allowance close to the zigzag. Press to set the stitches.

12 Mitred lace corner stitched using matching thread.

JOINING LACE

Invisible join *also repairing lace*

This technique of joining laces will provide an invisible join, which is impossible to duplicate by machine. The same technique is also used for repairing lace, by inserting a replacement piece. Wherever possible, joins are best worked around a lace motif, such as a flower and not through the mesh background. When creating a join at the hemline or around a sleeve, always complete the garment seams first. The lace will need to be overlapped on a complete motif, so be sure you have sufficient lace to form this overlap and create a circle of lace to match the size of the garment.

Suggested supplies

Needle
No. 10 crewel, no. 10 or no. 11 sharp

Pins
Extra fine glass head pins

Thread
Cotona no. 80, Madeira, Tanne no. 80
Lacis no. 100 or 120

1 Before commencing the lace join, plan the stitching path so there is at least 2cm (¾") overlap. Lightly mist both pieces with water and press with steam to shrink.

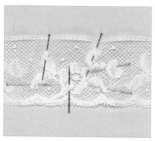

2 With right sides facing, pin one end of the lace on top of the other, matching as many points in the motif as possible.

3 Tack the laces together around the edge of the motif. Remove the pins.

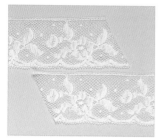

4 Secure a very fine matching thread within the lace motif and bring it to the front at the edge of the motif.

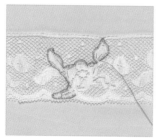

5 Work tiny blanket stitches around the lace motif, ensuring you secure both layers of lace.

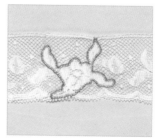

6 Steam and press the lace join to set the stitches.

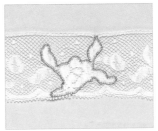

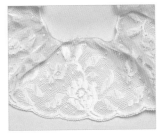

7 Lift the excess lace at one end over your finger. Trim close to the blanket stitching, clipping one thread at a time with very sharp, pointed scissors.

8 Turn the lace over and trim in the same manner.

9 Invisible join worked with matching thread.

NEATENING LACE ENDS

Turned hem

When finishing an opening edge, such as a neck edge with lace, the ends of the lace will need to be neatened. Leave 6mm (¼") of lace extending at each end.

1 Secure the thread in the fabric seam. Fold a double hem on the lace so the edge is level with the garment edge and press.

2 Using small stitches, handstitch along the inner foldline.

Roll and whip

1 Secure the thread in the fabric seam. Work a row of tiny running stitches along the raw edge of the lace.

2 Roll the end of the lace firmly over the needle, level with the finished garment edge, enclosing the running stitches.

3 Hold the roll firmly. Whip the rolled lace edge following steps 3–6 on pages 40–41. End off the thread securely close to the rolled edge.

ATTACHING LACE TO LACE

When working with two pieces of lace side by side, ensure that both have the right side facing up and the pattern in the lace matches before beginning to stitch. Use the very finest cotton thread available for an almost invisible join. When attaching lace to lace it is crucial that you do not apply any stretch from behind or hold back the lace in front of the presser foot. After zigzagging the laces, you may find ripples in the work. These are easily straightened by lightly applying spray starch and pressing with a steam iron. Always test and adjust the stitch length and width of the zigzag to suit your lace. The width of the stitch should just cover the lace headings.

Suggested machine settings and threads

Zigzag Stitch
W: 2.0–3.0
L: 1.0
Presser foot: edge-joining or all-purpose
Needle position: centre
Lace thread: Cotona no. 80 Lacis no. 120 or Tanne no. 80

1 With the right sides facing, position the lengths of lace side by side. under the foot. Begin stitching 1cm (⅜") from the end, ensuring the zigzag stitches covers both headings.

2 Continue stitching, ensuring the headings are butted closely together but do not overlap. The stitches should cover the headings, without encroaching on the net.

3 **Lace fabric.** Several pieces of lace can be joined in this manner to create wide insertions, edgings or 'lace fabric'.

JOINING HOLES IN LACE SEAMS

When joining laces with a zigzag seam, holes can easily occur if both lace headings do not get caught in the zigzag. It is easy and quick to mend by stitching along the section again. We used contrasting threads for photographic purposes.

1 One lace heading has slipped from the seam causing a hole.

2 Reduce the zigzag width slightly. Begin stitching a short distance above the hole in the seam and finish a short distance below, ensuring both edges are caught in the seam.

3 Trim the thread tails close to the lace.

ATTACHING CURVED LACE TO CURVED LACE

Lengths of lace can be shaped and joined to form collars, circles or curves. The lace is shaped using a template and a lace shaping board. Always shape the outermost length of lace first.

Preparation. Place your template over an ironing board or lace shaping board.

1 With the right sides facing and leaving 1.5cm (⅝") at the beginning, pin the outer edge of the lace along the traced line. Angle the pins over the lace heading and placing them 1cm (⅜") apart.

2 Ease out and gently pull the gimp thread at the upper edge of the lace at regular intervals until the lace lies flat.

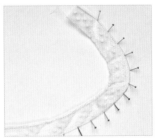

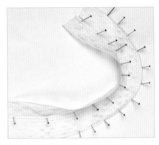

3 Smooth out the lace with your fingernail and press with the tip of the iron.

4 Position the second length of lace along the inside edge of the first and pin in place as before, ensuring the edges are butted together.

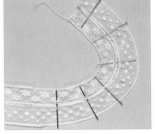

5 Shape the second piece of lace in the same manner, gently pulling the gimp thread. Smooth and press carefully as before.

6 Carefully free the pieces from the board, repositioning the pins through the laces only.

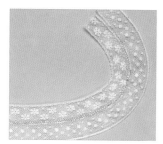

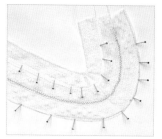

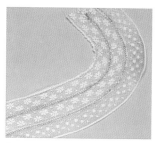

7 Begin stitching 1cm (⅜") from the end, ensuring the edges are butted together and the zigzag stitches covers both headings. Stitch, taking care not to stretch the shaped edges.

8 Reposition the joined laces on the board and pin in place. Pin and shape the third piece of lace following step 4 and 5.

9 Stitch the third piece of lace in place repeating steps 6–8.

CREATING LACE INSERTIONS

Lace insertions are not always available to exactly match a lace edging, or you may have lots of narrow edgings without a complementary insertion. You can create unique lace insertions or beading by joining lace edgings by hand. These delicate lace pieces work perfectly on Christening gowns or baby dresses and bonnets. Laces with a firm straight edge are the easiest to use. Use a finger shield when stitching the laces together.

Preparation. Lightly mist the lace with water and press with steam.

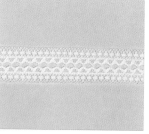
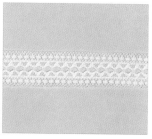

1 With right sides facing, place the two pieces of edging lace side by side with the tips of the lace scallops just touching.

Suggested supplies

Needle
no. 11 or no. 12 Sharp

Thread
Cotona no. 80, Madeira, Tanne no. 80
Lacis no. 100 or no. 120

Fine lace pins

Finger shield

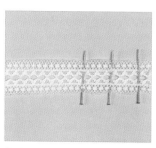

2 Gently pin a small section of lace together, ensuring the points or edges touch, but not overlap.

3 Secure a knotted thread at one end. Position the lace taut over your finger shield to begin stitching with a straight stitch to anchor.

4 Stitch with a small whipstitch over the edge of one lace piece. The stitches should be firm, but not tight.

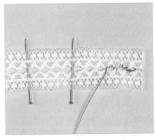
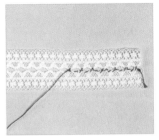

5 When you reach the point where two scallops meet, catch both lace points with a straight stitch.

6 Continue whipping along one side only until you reach the second scallop. Secure with a straight stitch from point to point.

7 Work a smocker's knot over the points at 2.5cm (1") intervals to prevent the lace from gathering.

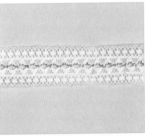
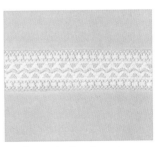
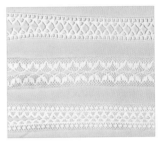

8 Continue in this manner, securing at regular intervals to ensure that you will be able to cut the insertion as necessary.

9 Alternatively, place the lace pieces together with the tips interlocking. The result is an entirely different lace insertion and a different width.

10 Examples of unique insertions stitched using matching thread.

INSERTING LACE

Flat fabric

This is a secure method for inserting lace into fabric. Test and adjust the width of your zigzag to suit your lace before you begin. If you are using the ¼" foot for the zigzag step, use the hand wheel for the first full stitch to prevent breaking the needle on the sides of the foot, if the width setting is too wide.

Suggested machine settings

Straight stitch
L: max 2.0
Presser foot: basic or ¼"
Needle position: centre

Zigzag stitch
W: 1.0–2.0, L: 0.75–1.0
Presser foot: straight stitch, ¼" or pintuck
Needle position: centre

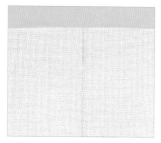

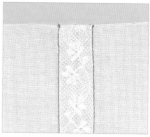

1 Remove two fabric threads along the centre of the lace placement. Highlight using a water-soluble fabric marker.

2 With right sides facing, centre the lace insertion over the marked line and tack in place through the centre of the lace or inside the lace headings.

3 Using small straight stitches and fine machine thread, stitch in the centre of each lace heading. Remove the tacking and press to set the stitches.

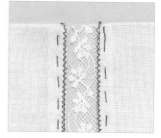

4 Wrong side. Using small blunt-nose or duckbill scissors, cut the fabric behind the lace using the pulled threads as a guide. Be careful not to cut the lace.

5 Press the seam allowances away from the lace, pushing with the side of the iron. Tack if necessary to hold in place.

6 Working from the right side, secure the lace with a tiny zigzag stitch that completely covers the lace heading. Gently press the stitches.

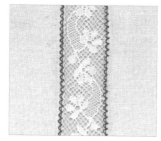

7 **Wrong side**. Trim the remaining seam allowance close to the zigzag. Hold the scissors flat with the fabric being cut resting over the tips of your fingers.

8 Completed lace insertion.

Hint

Decorative seams

For a more decorative finish, a machine pinstitch or hemstitch can be used along the edge of the lace instead of a zigzag stitch.

INSERTING LACE

Gathered fabric

This technique is used for applying a beading lace at the lower edge of a sleeve, gathering fabric to secure with an insertion or fabric casing.

Preparation Test and adjust the width of your zigzag to suit your lace before you begin.

1 Remove two fabric threads at the centre of the lace placement. Highlight using a fabric marker. Mark the width of the lace at the upper fabric edge.

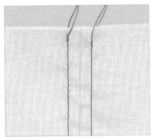

2 Stitch two rows of machine gathering 2mm (¹⁄₁₆") inside the marked width.

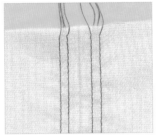

3 Stitch two more rows of machine gathering 2mm (¹⁄₁₆") outside the marked width.

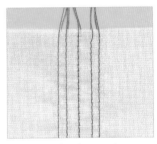

4 Stitch a final row of machine gathering along the marked centre line.

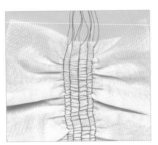

5 Pull the bobbin threads to gather the fabric to the required measurement. Spread the gathers evenly.

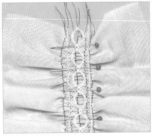

6 With the right sides facing, centre the lace over the gathers and pin.

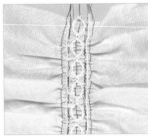

7 Tack the lace in place along both headings.

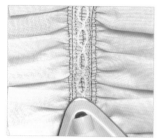 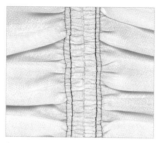 

8 Stitch along both headings. Remove the tacking. Press to set the stitches using the tip of the iron, taking care not to flatten the gathers.

9 Wrong side Remove the centre gathering thread only. Using a small pair of blunt-nose scissors, carefully cut along the centre of the fabric behind the lace.

10 Finger press the cut seam allowances away from the lace and tack in place.

11 Working from the right side, secure the insertion with a narrow zigzag. Remove the remaining tacking threads.

12 Remove any remaining gathering threads. On the wrong side trim the seam allowance close to the zigzag, holding the scissors flat and the fabric being cut over your finger tip.

13 Pressing With the wrong side facing, pin the lace section flat to your ironing board. Steam and press the lace, taking care not to flatten the gathers.

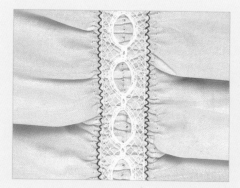

INSERTING LACE

Scallops

When creating scallops the curves can easily be distorted because you will be stitching largely on the bias grain. By working on a flat base, pinning and tacking to secure, it is possible to create beautiful scallops that maintain the look of smooth fabric.

Preparation The fabric and lace are prepared in a similar manner to attaching lace to scalloped edge. Prepare the scallop template as described on page 19 and draw or tack the scallop reference line and pivot lines.

Suggested machine settings

Straight stitch

L: max 2.0

Presser foot: basic or ¼"

Needle position: centre

Zigzag stitch

W: 1.0–2.0, L: 0.75–1.0

Presser foot: basic, ¼" or pintuck

Needle position: centre

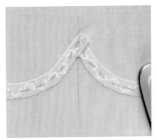

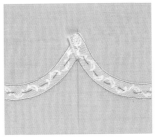

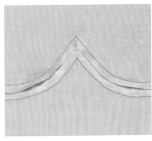

1 Position and shape the lace insertion following steps 1–6 on page 74. Tack the lace in place along the centre. Stitch along the lower lace heading, pivoting at the peak. Press to set the stitches.

2 Stitch along the upper lace heading, keeping the pleat free. The lace pleats are on the right side at the pivot point.

3 **Wrong side** Remove the tacking. Separate the layers and with small, blunt-nose scissors, cut the fabric along the centre behind the lace. Take care not to cut the lace.

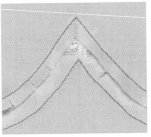

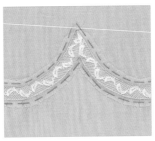

4 Clip into the curves at 1cm (⅜") intervals and into the pivot point at the top of each scallop. Remove a portion of the peak at the lower pivot point.

5 Press the seam allowances away from the lace, pushing with the side of the iron. Tack in place.

6 Push the lace pleat through to the wrong side at the pivot point. With right sides together, fold a scallop so the folded pleat lies flat.

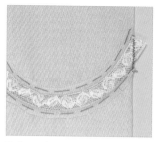 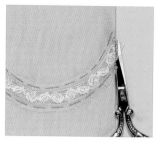 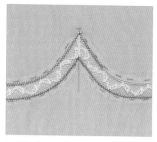

7 Straight stitch across the pleat. Stitch a narrow zigzag enclosing the straight stitches.

8 Trim the lace close to the zigzag.

9 Working from the right side, secure both sides of the insertion with a narrow zigzag, encasing the lace heading.

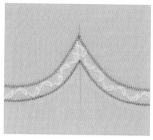  

10 Remove the tacking and press to set the stitches.

11 Wrong side Trim the remaining seam allowance close to the stitching, keeping the scissors flat against the fabric.

12 Inserted lace scallop worked using matching thread.

Hints

Insertion lace shapes

Shapes such as hearts, teardrops and diamonds or zigzag borders are all worked using the same method.

MITRING LACE INSERTION

Completing the mitre on the lace before inserting it into the fabric, enables you to create a precise corner.

Preparation. Mitre the lace following steps 1–5 on page 77. Mark the centre line for the lace position onto the fabric.

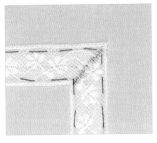

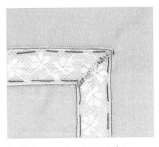

1 With right sides facing, centre the mitred lace over the marked line on the fabric. Tack the lace onto the fabric inside both headings.

2 Using a short straight stitch, machine stitch along both headings, pivoting at the corner points.

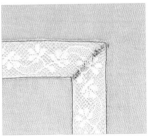

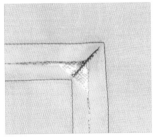

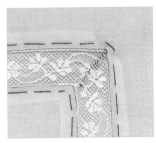

3 Remove the tacking. Press to set the stitches.

4 **Wrong side.** Separate the layers and carefully cut the fabric along the marked line. Cut diagonally into the outer corner. Cut the inner seam allowances to the inner pivot point.

5 Press the seam allowances away from the lace and tack in place.

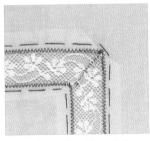

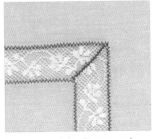

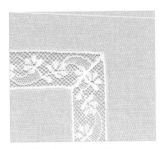

6 On the right side, stitch over the lace headings using a narrow zigzag to secure both sides of the lace.

7 **Wrong side.** Remove the tacking and press. Holding the scissors flat against the fabric, trim the seam allowances close to the stitching.

8 Mitred lace insertion stitched using matching thread.

Handworked edges and finishes

Decorative edgings can be worked over a corded edge, fabric fold, a rolled edge or seamline. The edges of sleeves, collars, cuffs, hems, pockets, openings, bonnets and booties are just some of the options. It is important that, when deciding on a handworked edging, you consider the suitability for everyday use, laundering and colourfastness.

BABY RICRAC EDGE

This edge treatment is perfect for enhancing collars, cuffs or front-button bands on baby garments.

Cotton ricrac is more suitable than polyester, as it will maintain its curved shape after being starched and pressed.

When working around curves ensure there is adequate ease to allow the ricrac to lie flat. This technique can be worked over your finger or pinned to a blocking board or heavy paper.

Suggested needles, threads and equipment

Needles
No.10 or no.11 sharps

Thread
Madeira Cotona
Tanne 80
No. 100 or Lacis no.
120 lace thread

Extra fine glass head pins

Finger shield or

blocking board

1 Attaching the ricrac
Prepare the fabric edge using your chosen method. Lay the ricrac along the edge. Lightly mist with spray starch and steam to shape the ricrac around a curved shape.

2 Secure the thread. Attach the first ricrac peak with a straight stitch, taking the needle to the back through the peak. Re-emerge through the same hole in the fabric.

3 Whip over the fabric edge to the next ricrac peak, ensuring the last whipping stitch is directly level with the second ricrac peak.

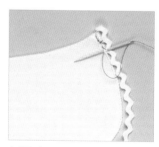

4 Work a straight stitch through the peak, bringing the needle to the front through the same hole in the fabric as the whipping stitch.

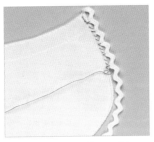

5 Secure 5–6 peaks in this manner. Work a smocker's knot on the fabric edge to secure the whipping stitches.

6 Continue in this manner, ensuring the ricrac peaks are butted against the fabric edge and do not underlap.

7 Collar piece with ricrac trim stitched with matching thread.

BABY RICRAC AND LACE EDGE

A ricrac edge can be further embellished with flat or gathered lace.

Preparation for flat lace Cut a piece of narrow lace edging that is longer than the ricrac trim. Pull the heading threads until the lace 'ripples' slightly and there is ample fullness around the curves.

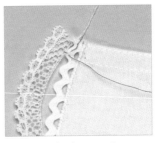

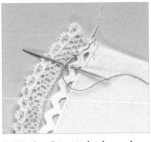

1 Lay the lace along the edge. Shape the lace around a curved shape by following the instructions on page 74 if required. Lightly mist and press.

2 Secure the lace to the ricrac within the seam allowance, working a straight stitch at the ricrac peak.

3 Work whipstitch along the lace heading to the next ricrac peak. Work a straight stitch into the peak, re-emerging through the same hole in the lace heading as the whipping stitch.

4 Continue attaching the lace to the ricrac in this manner.

5 Collar piece with ricrac and lace trim worked using matching thread.

6 **Gathered lace edge.** Cut the lace twice the length of the ricrac trim and gather to fit following the instructions on page 76. Attach the lace in the same manner as the flat lace.

BLANKET STITCH AND BUTTONHOLE STITCH EDGE

Buttonhole and blanket stitch are used for embellishing heirloom garments along bound necklines, collars and cuffs, around the yoke on a daygown or to highlight a front button band. Both these stitches can be worked as single or multiple rows or detached to form a scallop edge. The two stitches are both worked over the edge of the fabric, they are similar in appearance and easily confused.

Blanket stitch creates a smooth neatened edge. It is worked, beginning each stitch with the needle in the fabric, pointing towards the edge.

Buttonhole stitch creates a more solid edging as the stitch forms a row of 'purls' or 'knots' along the edge. It is worked, beginning each stitch with the needle off the edge, pointing towards the body of the fabric.

Suggested threads and needles

Thread
Coton à broder
Floche
No. 12 Perlé cotton
Stranded cotton

Needle
No. 8–10 crewel or No. 28 tapestry

Blanket stitch edge

A blanket stitch is made by positioning your work with the finished edge towards you and working horizontally from left to right. Left-handed stitchers will work from right to left.

Preparation Using a fine tip water-soluble marker, place dots along the prepared edge to mark the size and spacing of the stitches.

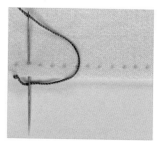

1 Secure the thread and bring it to the front through the finished edge.

2 Hold the thread under your thumb. Take the needle from front to back at the first mark, keeping the thread loop under the tip of the needle.

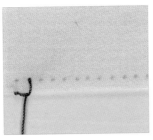

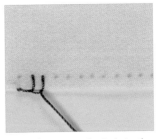

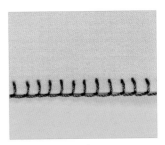

3 Pull the thread towards you, taking care not to pucker the fabric.

4 Work a second stitch in the same manner at the next marked point.

5 Continue in this manner along the edge, placing the stitches evenly side by side.

Buttonhole stitch edge

Buttonhole stitch is best stitched with the finished edge away from you, stitching horizontally from right to left. Keep the stitches evenly spaced and the knots positioned on the finished edge. Uniform tension is easier to maintain if the stitches are closer together.

Preparation. Using a fine water-soluble marker, place dots along the prepared edge to mark the size and spacing of the stitches.

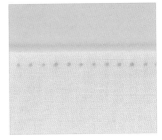

1 Secure the thread and bring it to the front at the finished edge.

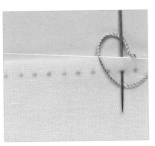

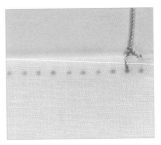

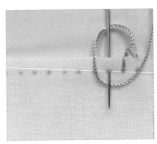

2 Loop the thread anti-clockwise. Take the needle from back to front at the first mark, keeping the thread under the needle.

3 Gently pull the thread away from the edge, forming a knot at the edge.

4 Move the thread over the fabric, forming a loop. Repeat step 3.

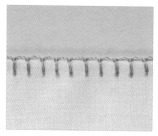

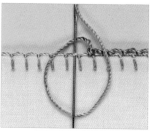

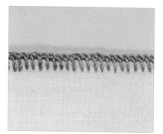

5 Continue in this manner along the edge.

6 **Wider edging** Work a second row of buttonhole stitch, working each stitch into a stitch on the previous row.

7 Firm edging. Keeping the stitches close together, creates a neat, firm edge.

BLANKET STITCH OR BUTTONHOLE STITCH

Joining a new thread

It is important to frequently change to a new thread to achieve a good finish. The new thread is joined in a similar manner for blanket stitch and buttonhole stitch. We used contrasting threads for photographic purposes.

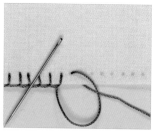

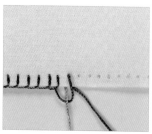

1 Work the last stitch, but do not pull taut. Unthread the needle.

2 Secure the new thread. Emerge through the same hole as the old thread tail and through the thread loop.

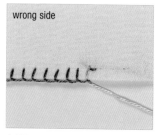

wrong side

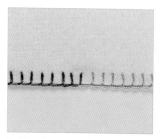

3 Pull the old thread taut around the emerging thread.

4 **Wrong side** Re-thread the old thread and secure on the wrong side.

5 Continue stitching.

> Hint
>
> **Multiple rows**
>
> Secure the thread tails when stitching multiple rows by weaving the thread through the back of the buttonhole stitches and securing at the edge of the fabric.

BUTTONHOLE STITCH TO ENTREDEUX

Adding one or more rows of buttonhole stitches to an entredeux edge creates a very tailored finish, and an opportunity to add colour in your thread choice.

We used contrasting threads for photographic purposes.

1 Prepare the entredeux edge in a similar manner to the instructions on page 32, ensuring ample ease around any curves.

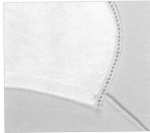

2 Secure the thread and bring it to the front through the first hole in the entredeux.

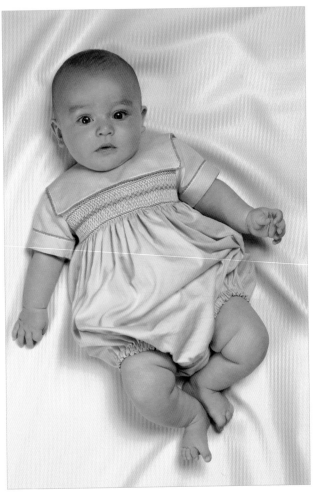

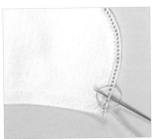

3 Work a buttonhole stitch taking the needle from back to front through the next hole.

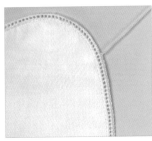

4 Continue along the entredeux, working a buttonhole stitch into each hole and rotating the garment piece as you stitch.

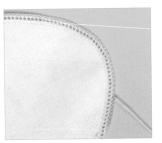

5 **Second row** Stitching in the same direction, work a second row of buttonhole stitches into the first, taking care not to pull the thread tight within the curved area.

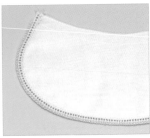

6 Completed double buttonhole stitch edge, worked using matching thread.

BUTTONHOLE STITCH WITH BEADS

Petite beads can be used to add final detail to a buttonhole or blanket stitch edge. We used contrasting thread to attach the beads for photographic purposes.

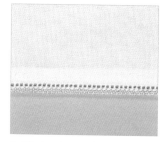

1 Work a buttonhole edge, working the required number of rows, following the instructions on page 94–95.

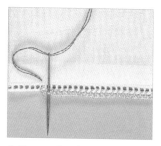

2 Secure the thread within the seam allowance at the left hand edge. Take the needle from front to back through the first buttonhole stitch.

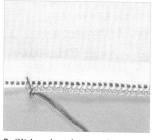

3 Slide a bead onto the thread. Rest the bead against the edge and work a stitch through the buttonhole stitch in the same direction once more.

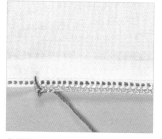

4 Taking the needle from front to back, whip into the following two buttonhole stitches.

5 Stitch a second bead in place in the same manner as before.

6 Continue to whip stitch along the edge attaching a bead at every second buttonhole stitch.

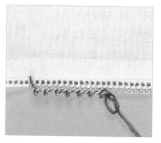

7 For every six or seven beads, secure the thread with a smocker's knot next to the bead.

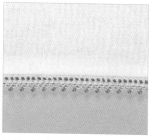

8 Beaded edge worked with matching thread.

BLANKET STITCH SCALLOPS

Scallops can be worked directly onto a neatened edge or into entredeux. To work scallops onto a neatened edge, mark the spacing of the scallops along the edge using a water-soluble fabric marker.

We used contrasting threads for photographic purposes.

1 Prepare the fabric edge using your chosen method.

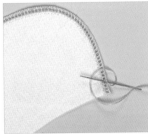

2 Secure the thread within the seam allowance. Using a tapestry needle, work a buttonhole stitch into an entredeux hole (or first marked point) aligned with the garment seam line.

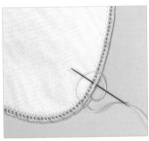

3 Work buttonhole stitches into every third hole of the entredeux, rotating the fabric piece as you work.

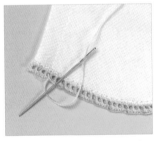

4 Secure a new thread and work a blanket stitch into the first loop.

5 Work the required number of the blanket stitches to cover the loop. Count the number of stitches so all subsequent scallops will be even.

6 To anchor the scallop, slide the needle from back to front through the anchoring stitch of first row.

7 Work the second scallop in the same manner, counting the stitches.

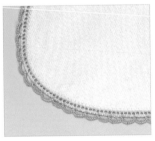

8 Continue working an even number of blanket stitches into each loop in this manner.

BULLION SCALLOP EDGE

This is a fabulous edging for bound necklines, collars and cuffs, around the yoke of a daygown or to highlight a front button band. The length of the bullion scallops should be 6mm–1cm (¼"–⅜") depending on the garment and the fabric weight. Always work a small sample to test the spacing before you begin.

1 Using a fine water-soluble fabric marker, place dots along the prepared edge at the required intervals.

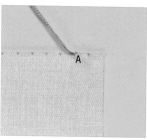

2 Knot the thread and bring it to the front through the fold or seam at the second mark, A. Work a tiny back stitch to secure.

Suggested threads and needles

Needle
No. 8–no. 10 milliner's

Thread
Floche, no. 80 tatting thread stranded cotton or silk (2–3 strands)

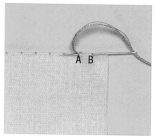

3 Working from right to left, insert the needle at the first mark, B and re-emerge at A. Leave the needle in the fabric.

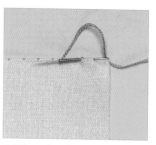

4 Wrap the thread around the tip of the needle. Push the wraps together on the needle. The width of the wraps should be slightly longer than the distance between two marks.

Hints

Bullion scallops

1 Make one or two practice scallops before marking your garment, to ensure that they are the desired size.

2 Make note of the number of wraps and from which end of the skein your needle was threaded. These minor points make a big difference to smooth bullion knots.

3 Use a length of thread no longer than 30–40cm (12–15"). Change to a new thread after six or seven scallops.

4 Despite your best effort, scallops will not be uniform in size and fullness. It is the completed row that impresses.

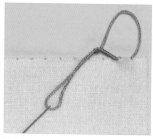

5 Holding the wraps securely between your finger and thumb, begin to pull the needle and thread through the wraps.

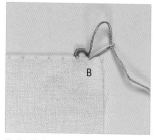

6 Pull the thread through. Take the needle to the back at the end of the bullion scallop, B.

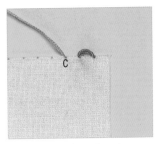

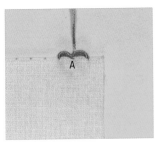

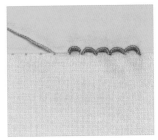

7 Bring the thread to the front at the third marked dot, C.

8 Work a second bullion scallop in the same manner, stitching into the same hole at A.

9 Continue stitching bullion scallops along the edge in the same manner.

CROCHET SCALLOPED EDGING

Alacy edging is created by using the holes in the entredeux as the foundation for working this simple scalloped crochet edge.

Preparation Use a chenille needle to secure the crochet thread within the seam allowance on the back of the piece to be worked close to the first entredeux hole.

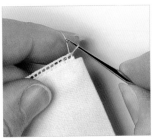

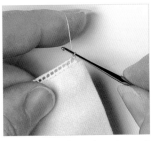

1 Take the crochet hook through the first entredeux hole. Wrap the thread from back to front around the hook. Pull the loop through to the front.

2 Wrap the thread again and pull through the loop to secure the stitch.

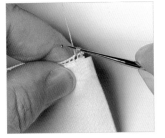

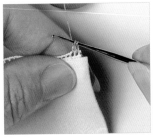

3 **First treble stitch** Wrap the thread as before. Take the hook through the next entredeux hole to the left. Pull the thread through.

4 Wrap the thread from front to back around the hook and pull through the first two stitches on the hook.

5 Wrap the thread again and pull through the remaining two stitches on the hook.

6 Repeat steps 3–5 to work a further three treble stitches into the same entredeux hole.

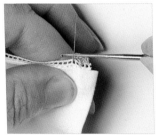

7 **Double crochet** Take the hook through the next hole and pull the thread through to the front. There are two stitches on the hook.

8 Wrap the thread from back to front around the hook and pull through both stitches to form a double crochet stitch.

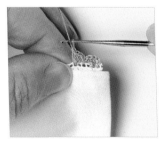

9 Work four treble stitches into the next hole as before.

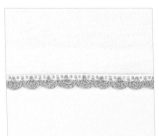

10 Continue working treble stitch and double crochet to the end of the entredeux.

DECORATIVE THREAD REPLACEMENT

Suggested threads,
ribbons and needles

Thread
Floche, stranded cotton

Ribbon
2–3mm (1/16"–1/8") silk ribbon

Needle
Bodkin, no. 26 or 28 tapestry

An interesting detail is to replace several fabric threads for one of a contrasting colour and texture. It is an effective method for adding detail to collars, yokes, sleeve bands, cuffs or ruffles. This technique must be worked on a fabric that is woven coarsely enough to permit the threads to be drawn out. Wool, cotton, linen and some silks are suitable.

Patterns are created by weaving contrasting thread or ribbon over and under the remaining fabric threads in a chosen pattern.

The weft thread count will most likely be different to the warp thread count. You may prefer to weave using a visual measurement instead of counting threads.

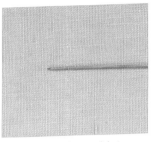

1 Carefully lift one fabric thread and gently draw it from the weave. If the thread breaks, ease the tail out again using the needle.

2 Continue to remove more threads in the same manner until the area is wide enough to accommodate the replacement thread or ribbon.

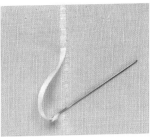

3 Thread a tapestry needle or bodkin with thread or ribbon and weave along the row in your chosen sequence.

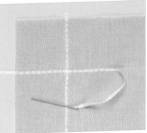

4 Continue until the entire row is filled. If weaving perpendicular rows, begin at the intersecting point to ensure correct sequence.

5 Several rows of thread replacement can be worked to create a pattern.

FAGGOTING

Or twisted insertion

Faggoting is a decorative embroidery stitch used to join two separate sections while creating design and character to the negative space. It makes a decorative finish and can be used to attach lace or rouleau to a collar edge and hemline, lace insertion between two straight fabric sections or for a decorative effect when used with silk ribbon or baby ricrac. The faggoted seam can be a style line that you create within the garment or an actual construction seam. In either case the edges being joined must be finished before you begin.

Suggested threads and needles

Threads
No. 12 perlé cotton no. 50 machine embroidery cotton (waxed), no. 80 tatting thread

Needles
No. 7 or no. 8 crewel no. 28 tapestry

1 Preparation Tack the prepared garment piece to stiff paper. Draw a line parallel to the finished edge, leaving a 3–6mm (⅛"–¼") spacing.

2 Shape and gather if necessary the lace (or other trim) to fit the marked line and tack securely in place on the paper template.

3 Faggoting Secure the thread on the edge of the garment piece.

4 Pick up a few threads at the edge of the lace. Ensure the thread loop is under the needle.

5 Pull the thread through. With the thread behind the needle, pick up a few threads at the edge of the garment 3mm (⅛") from the secured thread.

6 Pull the thread through. Take a stitch as before through the lace 3mm (⅛") from the first stitch.

Faggoting

Faggoting most likely developed as an extension of the antique seam where 19th century linen fabric was too narrow for household linens and was joined selvedge-to-selvedge by means of a closed, flat seam. This later came to resemble hemstitching and its bundles of threads.

FAGGOTED INSERTION – *continued*

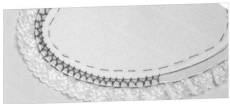

7 Continue along the garment edge, alternating the stitches. Adjust the spacing of the stitches on sharper curves, to maintain even stitches.

8 **Starting a new thread** Secure the new thread inconspicuously in the garment edge. Pass the thread through the fold and resume stitching the same way.

9 Clip the tacking on the wrong side of the paper and remove the garment piece. Lightly spray starch and steam to set the stitches.

10 Sample worked using matching thread.

HEMSTITCH

This is a drawn thread stitch, where threads are removed from the fabric in one direction and the remaining threads are secured in bundles. It is both decorative and functional, as it secures a hem while providing detailed embellishment. Because of the tension applied during stitching, the thread used must be strong and smooth, and relative to the weight of fabric.

Thread bundles secured evenly at both ends are known as ladder hemstitch and when secured in alternate bundles, serpentine or zigzag hemstitch.

Suggested fabrics, threads and needles

Fabrics
Batiste, fine linen, lawn or organdie

Threads
No. 12 perlé cotton, no. 25 Coton à Broder, no. 60 mercerized cotton or stranded cotton.

Needles
No. 7 or no. 8 crewel
No. 10 or no. 11 sharp
No. 28 tapestry

DRAWING THE THREAD

According to the type of fabric being used, the number of threads to be drawn out from the weft and warp directions is likely to vary. Measure the distance, rather than counting threads. Use a fine machine needle as it is stronger and has a sharper point, perfect for feeling and lifting the threads.

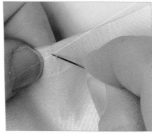

1 Using a sharp needle, carefully ease the end of one thread from the fabric near the raw edge.

2 Very gently pull the thread as close to the fabric as possible, withdrawing it from the fabric. The fabric will gather as you pull.

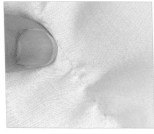

3 When the thread breaks, gently ease out the broken end at the break point. Position the taut thread and slightly gathered fabric over the sensitive pad of your fingers.

4 Press the point of the needle over the threads to locate the broken end and lift from the fabric. Ease remaining end out of the weave and continue drawing out the thread.

5 Draw out several adjacent threads until the band of removed threads is the required width.

HEMSTITCHING

Hemstitch is worked from left to right on the wrong side of the fabric, leaving only tiny stitches visible on the right side.

You can count the number of threads in each bundle on coarse fabric however on fine fabrics gauge the width by eye.

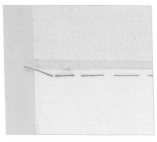

1 **Prepare the hem** Fold and press a double hem and tack in place.

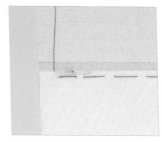

2 Secure the thread inside the fold. Take the needle between the layers of the hem, and emerge in the upper fold.

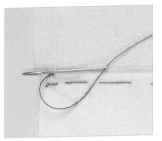

3 With the thread below the needle, slide the needle from right to left under the required number of threads.

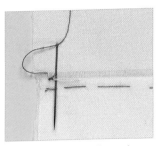

4 Pull the thread through, drawing up the bundle. Take a vertical stitch through all layers on the right hand side of the bundle, catching 2–3 threads of the hem fold.

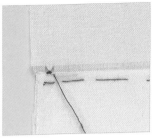

5 Pull the thread through until the bundle of threads is tightly grouped together.

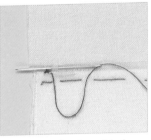

6 Keeping the thread below, slide the needle from right to left behind the next bundle of threads.

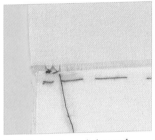

7 Pull the thread through, drawing up the bundle. Work a small stitch in the same manner as step 4. Draw up the second bundle of threads.

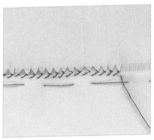

8 Continue working stitches following steps 3–5.

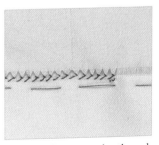

9 To finish, secure the thread close to the hem fold just below the last bundle.

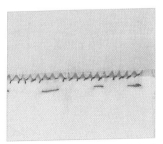

10 **Right side** A tiny vertical stitch is visible between each thread bundle.

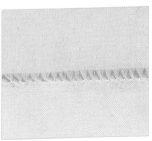

11 Hem stitch worked using matching thread.

LADDER HEMSTITCH

Stitching along the opposite side of the drawn thread bundles, further secures the bundles and creates a more decorative hemline. Work the first row of hemstitch following the instructions on the page 105.

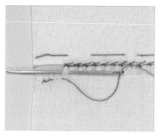

1 Turn the work upside down. Pick up the first thread bundle, sliding the needle from right to left.

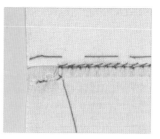

2 Work a vertical stitch on the right hand side of the bundle, catching 2–3 fabric threads.

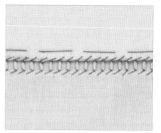

3 Continue working hem stitch around the same thread bundles as the first row.

SERPENTINE OR ZIGZAG HEMSTITCH

Work the first row of hemstitch following the instructions on pages 105–106.

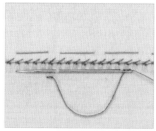

1 Turn the fabric upside down. Pick up half the first bundle of threads for the first stitch.

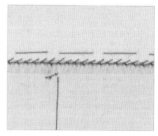

2 Draw up the half bundle and work a vertical stitch next to the bundle, catching 2–3 fabric threads.

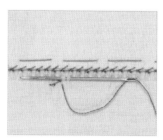

3 Pick up the first half of the second bundle and the remaining half of the first bundle of threads.

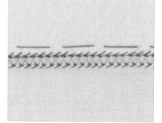

4 Continue grouping alternate bundles in this manner creating a zigzag pattern of bars.

Hemstitch

As far back as medieval times, drawn thread embroideries were done on coarse linen with a thread of the same thickness. Most examples of drawn thread work are stitched on white or natural fabric with matching threads, but examples of coloured stitching can be found in many east European national costumes and household items.

PALESTRINA KNOT EDGE

Suggested threads and needles

Threads
No. 8 or no. 12 perlé cotton
Stranded cotton or silk (2–4 strands)

Needles
No. 8 crewel
No. 28 tapestry

Palestrina Knot forms a decorative edge that resembles fine piping. Worked as an edging the method of working the stitch varies slightly from the traditional stitch used for surface embroidery.

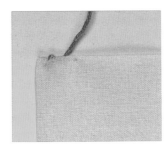

1 Secure the thread and bring it to the front through the folded or neatened edge at the starting point.

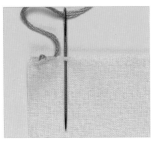

2 Take a small stitch from back to front through the edge of the fabric.

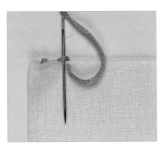

3 With the thread to the right, slide the needle under the previous stitch without catching the fabric.

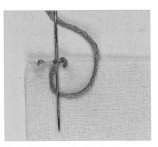

4 Pull through. Slide the needle under the first stitch without piercing the fabric, ensuring the thread loop is under the tip of the needle.

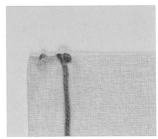

5 Pull the thread through towards you to form a knot.

Hints

1 Always work in one direction, especially on pairs of collars so identical knots are maintained.

2 Keeping the knots close together, makes it easier to maintain an even tension and create a continuous line of texture or colour.

3 To tighten the tension of each stitch, gently pull on the working thread close to the fabric, not at the end of your thread length. This will allow you to feel when the knot is firm and will prevent over-tightening of the knots. Too much tension as you tighten each stitch will cause your fabric edge to pucker.

4 When working over a seam, pick up the top layer of fabric only, as this will help the knots sit to the front of your garment.

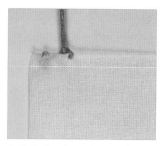
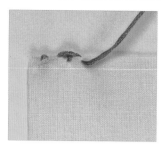
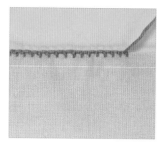

6 Pull the thread away from you to position the knot on the edge of the fabric.

7 Bring the thread through the fabric edge at the position for the next stitch.

8 Continue repeating steps 3–7, forming the knotted edge. Change the thread before it becomes worn.

RUCHED FABRIC EDGE

Ruching provides an attractive way to gather ruffles for hem or sleeve finishes, or the ruffle on a baby bonnet. By incorporating this technique, very simple garments can be transformed into an heirloom to treasure. Suitable fabrics for ruching include Swiss embroidered edging, fine batiste and voile, silk batiste and cotton netting.

For the best result use a finger shield and/or blocking board.

Preparation. Neaten the fabric edge using your chosen method.

Cut the fabric or trim to be shirred two to three times longer than the finished length.

Suggested threads
and needles

Threads
Cotton covered polyester for gathering
Mettler 60/2 or DMC 50 for attaching

Needle
No. 10 or no. 11 sharp

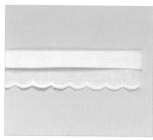
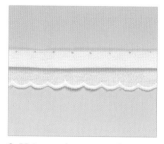

1 Fold a 1cm (⅜") double hem along one edge, enclosing the raw edge and press. Fold the fabric to the wrong side for gentle ruched scallops, and to the right side for a more defined look.

2 Using a sharp pencil or fine water-soluble marker, mark the upper folded edge at 1cm (⅜") intervals.

3 Mark along the opposite folded edge halfway between the previous marks.

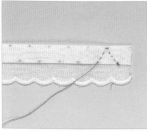

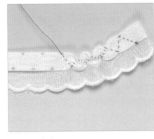

4 Secure the thread and work running stitch in a zigzag line between the marks from one folded edge to the other. Do not stitch over the edge.

5 Stitch between ten to twelve marks. Pull the thread to gather and form scallops.

6 Continue in this manner to the end of the edging, drawing up the gathers at regular intervals.

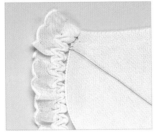

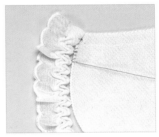

7 With right sides facing, lay the ruched edging along the fabric edge to measure the exact length.

8 Secure the first peak formed in the ruched edging to the fabric edge with a straight stitch.

9 Whip stitch over the fabric edge. At the next peak, work a straight stitch, through the peak re-emerging through the same hole in the fabric as the whipping stitch.

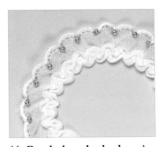

10 Continue stitching along the edge, working a straight stitch into every peak in the same manner. Ruched Swiss edging attached using matching thread.

11 **Beaded ruched edge** A ruched Swiss edging can be embellished with beads along the edge. Work running stitch along the scalloped edge and stitch a bead in place at each peak.

Hint

Attaching ruched edging

To prevent the ruched edging from cupping along a curved edge, always ensure there is more fullness around the curved area.

RUCHED RIBBON EDGE

Ruching silk ribbon creates a gently scalloped trim. It adds a delicate finish on collar and cuff edges, used as an insertion into yokes, over a neck binding or used as a ruffle on a baby bonnet or daygown. Use a finger shield and/or blocking board to achieve the best result.

Preparation. Neaten the fabric edge using your chosen method. Cut the silk ribbon two to three times longer than the finished edge.

1 Mark along one ribbon edge at 1cm (⅜") intervals. Place marks along the opposite edge halfway between the previous marks. Secure a thread at one end of the ribbon.

Suitable ribbons, threads and needles

Ribbons
4–7mm wide (⅛–³⁄₁₆") silk ribbon

Threads
Cotton covered polyester for gathering
DMC 50 or Mettler 60/2 for attaching

Needle
No. 10 or no. 11 sharp

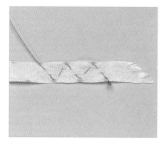

2 Work running stitch in a zigzag line between the marks, taking the stitches to the edge, but not over it. Do not make the stitches too small, as the ribbon will not draw up neatly.

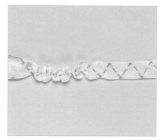

3 Stitch between ten to twelve marks. Pin the end of the ribbon to a blocking board. Draw up the threads to gather and form scallops.

4 Continue in this manner to the end of the ribbon, drawing up the gathers at regular intervals.

Hint

When attaching ruched ribbon around the curves of a collar, be sure to ease the running stitches and not allow them to pull tight, causing the ruching to flip up.

5 With right sides facing, lay the ruched ribbon along the fabric edge to measure the exact length.

6 Using fine thread, attach the first peak formed in the shirred ribbon to the fabric edge with a straight stitch.

7 Whip stitch over the fabric edge to the next peak in the ribbon.

8 Work a straight stitch taking the thread to the back through the peak and to the front through the same hole in the fabric as the whipping stitch.

9 Continue whip stitching along the edge, working a straight stitch into every ribbon peak. Secure the stitches with a smocker's knot on the fabric edge for every six or seven peaks.

10 Ruched ribbon edge stitched using matching thread.

RUCHED RIBBON AND LACE EDGE

Adding lace to a ruched ribbon edge makes a beautiful finish for collars and cuffs.

Preparation. Shape the lace around a curved shape by following the instructions on page 74 if required. Lightly mist and press.

1 With right side facing, lay the lace along the edge. Secure the lace to the ribbon within the garment seam allowance.

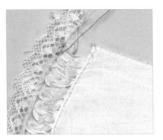

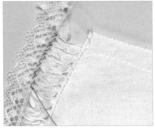

2 Whip stitch along the lace heading to the next ribbon peak. Work a straight stitch, into the peak re-emerging through the same hole in the lace heading.

3 Continue attaching the lace to the ruched ribbon in this manner. Secure the stitching with a smocker's knot after every six or seven peaks.

4 Ruched ribbon edge with lace trim worked using matching thread.

Construction techniques

General garment construction techniques are used for much heirloom sewing. However, some techniques are more appropriate than others to accomodate the delicate fabrics and trims.

BUTTONS AND BUTTONHOLES

Placement

To provide strength and stability, always work buttonholes and buttons onto three thicknesses of fabric, or two thicknesses of fabric plus interfacing. Buttonholes have to withstand strain when the garment is worn so it is important to position the buttonholes in the direction of the greatest strain to prevent the garment from unfastening too easily.

Horizontal buttonholes are the most secure. They are stitched at a right angle to the opening edge, with the first bartack positioned 2mm (1/16") past the button placement line.

Vertical buttonholes are most often used with a placket or button band, such as on a shirt or with the shoulder buttons on a petticoat, pinafore or overalls. They are placed directly on the button placement line and the top of the buttonhole is 3mm (1/8") above the mark for the centre of the button.

The distance between the button and buttonhole placement line and the opening edge should be at least equal to the diameter of the button. If the button size is changed, the distance between the placement line and the opening edge must be altered accordingly. To ensure the garment closes correctly, the buttons and buttonholes must be placed so the centre front or back of the garment piece is aligned when the garment is buttoned.

girl's front   girl's back

boy's front   boy's back

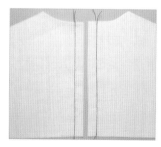

1 Determine the centre front or back placement and tack or rule a line.

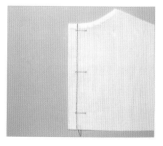

2 Mark the placement for the button-holes by tacking or using a suitable marker.

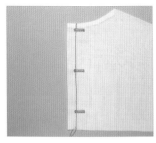

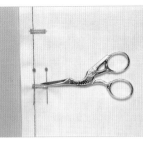

3 Stitch the buttonholes, using your chosen method, beginning each at the end closest to the garment edge.

4 Using a seam ripper, chisel or small sharp scissors, cut open each button-hole. Place a pin at each end of the buttonhole to prevent cutting into the bartack.

5 Lap the buttonholed piece over the corresponding garment piece, aligning the centre lines.

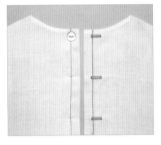

6 Place a pin through the end of each buttonhole on the centre placement line.

7 Ease the pins through the button-holes without removing them from the fabric. Mark the pin positions with a suitable marker. Attach the buttons at the marked points.

8 Completed buttons and buttonholes.

Hints

The direction of the lap varies for girls and boys and if the garment is front or back opening.

cutting buttonholes Always stitch all the buttonholes before cutting them open.

novelty buttons These can be difficult to button and require an oversized buttonhole because of their odd shape or thickness. They are best used as decoration only and should be attached to the garment over a snap fastener or hook and eye.

shank buttons Avoid using buttons with a high shank on the back of garments intended for babies or toddlers, as the shank will press into the child's back when laying down.

HANDWORKED BUTTONHOLE

Buttonholes stitched by hand add an extra special touch and are particularly suited to delicate fabrics. Mark the buttonhole on the fabrics, adding extra lines to mark the width.

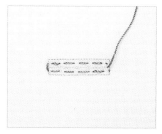

1 Work running stitch around the buttonhole finishing at the right hand end. Cut the opening. Bring the thread to the front through the opening.

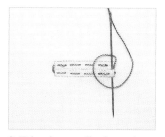

2 Take the needle through the opening and emerge on the lower line. Wrap the thread anti-clockwise behind the eye and then the tip of the needle.

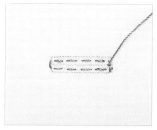

3 Pull the thread through, bringing it towards you and then up towards the opening, until the knot settles on the cut edge.

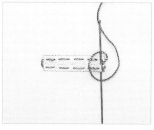

4 Take the needle through the opening again and emerge next to the previous stitch. Wrap the thread around the needle as before.

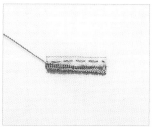

5 Continue in this manner until you reach the end of the opening. Keep the stitches as close as possible.

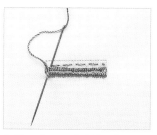

6 **First bartack** Take the needle through the opening and emerge close to the previous stitch on the lower line.

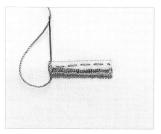

7 Work several stitches across the end. Take the needle to the back at the upper edge.

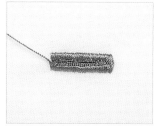

8 Turn the fabric upside down. Work buttonhole stitch as before, across the remaining long side.

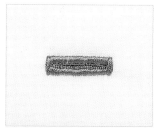

9 Make a bartack as in steps 6 and 7. Take the thread to the back, weave through the stitching on the back to secure and trim.

MACHINE STITCHED BUTTONHOLES

There are two ways in which a machine-worked buttonhole may be made.

Automatic buttonholes are stitched using a fully automatic buttonhole foot. A button is placed into the back of the foot and the machine gauges the correct buttonhole length to fit.

Semi-automatic buttonholes are stitched using the buttonhole foot and the pre-set buttonhole settings on your machine.

Machine settings

Refer to your sewing machine manual and stitch samples to achieve the size and look you want. Check your machine manual to determine if the width of each buttonhole bead can be reduced. Always stitch your practice buttonholes on the same fabric and number of layers as used for the garment.

Buttonhole samples

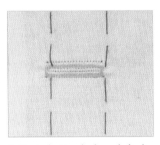

1 Basic buttonhole – default settings.

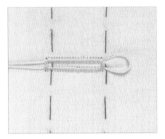

2 Basic corded buttonhole – width reduced from 4.0 to 3.5.

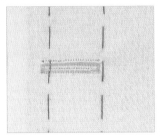

3 Small buttonhole – default settings.

Hint

Stabilising buttonhole

On fine fabrics, position a length of fine tracing paper underneath the fabric to help reduce puckering. This is easily pulled away when all buttonholes are complete.

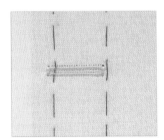

4 Small buttonhole – width reduced from 3.0 to 2.5.

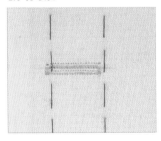

5 Small buttonhole stitched with tracing paper backing.

THREAD LOOP

When a front or back button closure is fastened, a small flap of the bodice will extend beyond the first button. Adding a tiny button and thread loop or hook and eye to fasten this extension helps the neckline to sit correctly.

The length of the thread loop is slightly less than the diameter of the button.

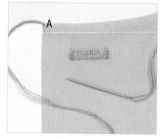

1 Using a long doubled thread, bring the needle to the front at the top of the folded edge, A. Work one or two tiny back stitches to secure.

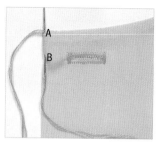

2 Sliding the needle between the fabric layers, take the needle from B to A. The distance between A and B is slightly less than the diameter of the button.

3 Pull the needle through, leaving a small loop. Take the needle from B to A again, forming a four-thread loop.

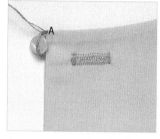

4 Test the loop for size by slipping the button through the loop. Adjust if necessary. Secure the thread at A with tiny back stitches.

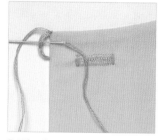

5 **Blanket stitch** Take the needle under the loop and over the thread.

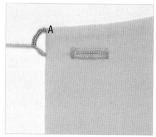

6 Pull the stitch firmly towards A. Continue working blanket stitch over the loop, packing the stitches together firmly.

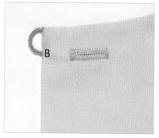

7 When the loop is covered, secure the thread at B.

8 Attach the button to correspond with the loop.

Hems

In heirloom sewing, hems are often used to create a design feature with the addition of tucks or trims. Tucks add interest to the hem of a skirt but must be positioned carefully to achieve the correct balance.

HEMMING INTO TUCK

This technique not only makes a pretty hemline tuck, but the hem is invisibly secured at the same time. The size of the hem and tuck can be adjusted by varying the size of the folds you make.

Determine the finished length of the skirt. Add the hem depth and three times the tuck size.

For example: Add 17.5cm (7") to allow for a 10cm (4") hem with a 2.5cm (1") tuck. Cut the skirt to include this additional length.

Place the garment on the ironing board with right side facing up. Measure the depth of the hem adding the width of the tuck. Pin and press following steps 1–4 on page 57. Tack the folds if necessary.

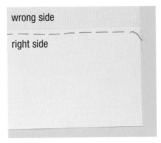

1 Fold under the hem with added tuck allowance to the wrong side. Pin in place and press the fold. Tack close to the raw edge if necessary.

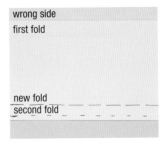

2 Fold the hem allowance again, enclosing the raw edge. Pin and press. Tack if required.

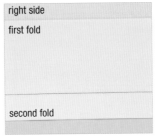

3 With the right side facing, stitch the tuck the required distance from the second fold. Remove the tacking and press to set the stitches.

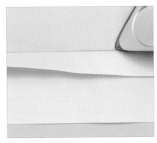

4 Unfold the hem. Press the hem and the tuck downwards, using the side of the iron to make a smooth seamline.

HEM TUCK

A sequence of complementary tucks work well if they are added above the hem tuck, and overlapped slightly so the stitching lines do not show. These tucks are also known as growth tucks as they are easy to release as the child grows. Determine the depth of the tuck and add twice this measurement to the length of the skirt.

right side

1 Measure up from the raw edge to the point at which the tuck is to be stitched.

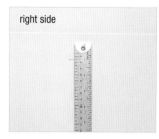

right side

2 Measure down the depth of the tuck and mark with a pin.

right side

3 Take the measurement from the marked point to the raw edge.

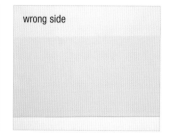

wrong side

4 Working from the wrong side, fold at this measurement around the hem. Press the fold.

wrong side

5 Stitch the tuck the determined width from the folded edge. Press to set the stitches.

right side

6 Unfold the fabric and press the tuck towards the hemline.

HEM TUCK WITH SWISS EDGING

Narrow tuck

This is a wonderful hem treatment when you need to lengthen a dress. It also gives a nice finish to baby dresses and Christening gowns.

Preparation Determine the finished skirt length. Measure the width of the edging. Subtract this width from the finished skirt length and mark. To allow for a 1cm (⅜") seam allowance and a 1cm (⅜") tuck, add 3cm to the marked length. Trim at this measurement. Measure the circumference of the skirt. Add a 2cm (¾") seam allowance to each end of the Swiss embroidered edging. Join the edging into a circle with a small French seam. Mark the half and quarter points on the skirt and the embroidered edging.

Hint

Make a test hemline tuck to be sure the tuck is covering the first seam. It may be necessary to move the needle position slightly to the left to ensure a hidden seam.

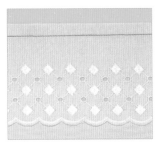

1 With right sides together and matching raw edges, place the edging onto the fabric and stitch a 1cm (¾") seam. Press to set the stitches.

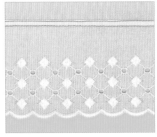

2 Neaten the seam allowance using a narrow self bound seam following the instructions on page 139.

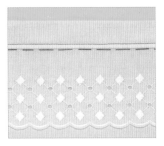

3 From the seamline measure and mark the foldline of the tuck. Fold the fabric with wrong sides together along the marked line. Press and tack.

4 Stitch a 1cm (⅜") seam. Remove the tacking and press to set the stitches.

5 Press the tuck towards the edging, pushing firmly with the side of the iron. The folded edge of the tuck should just cover the seamline.

6 Decorative seam The tuck stitch-line can be embellished with whip stitches using matching or contrasting embroidery thread.

HEM TUCK WITH SWISS EDGING

Wide tuck

When choosing an edging with a wider batiste heading above the embroidery a deeper tuck can be added.

Measure the depth of batiste above the embroidery. This will be the depth of the tuck.

Determine the finished length of the skirt. Add twice the tuck depth and a 6mm (¼") seam allowance to this measurement.

1 With right sides together and matching raw edges, place the edging over the fabric and stitch a 6mm (¼") seam.

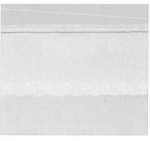

2 Press to set the stitches and grade the seam allowance with the smaller allowance on the garment.

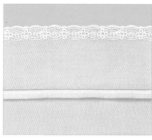

3 Open out the edging and press the seam allowances towards the fabric.

4 On the right side measure and mark the foldline for the tuck from the seamline.

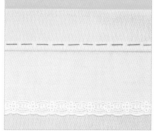

5 With wrong sides together, press and tack the fold.

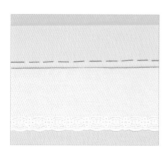

6 Stitch in the ditch between the fabric and the embroidered edging, enclosing the seam within the tuck. Press to set the stitches.

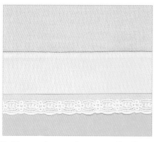

7 Press the tuck towards the embroidered edging.

8 Decorative seam The tuck stitch-line can be embellished with whipping stitches using matching or contrasting embroidery thread.

NARROW HEM

Suggested machine settings
Presser foot: edge-joining
Needle position: just left of centre

A narrow hem is often used for hemming full or sheer garments such as nightgowns, hem linings or for a curved hem, where a deeper hem is not suitable. It is also used on the edges of ruffles.

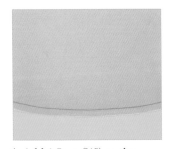

1 Add 1.5cm (⅝") to the finished length. Staystitch 1cm (⅜") from the raw edge, through a single thickness of fabric.

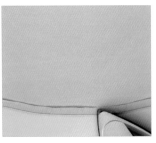

2 Fold the hem to the wrong side along the stitchline, ensuring the stitches are turned to the wrong side. Using the tip of the iron press the hem and steam the excess fabric into place.

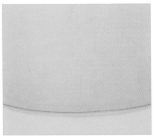

3 From the right side, machine stitch not more than 3mm (⅛") from the folded edge. Press to set the stitches.

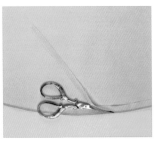

4 Working from the wrong side and using very sharp scissors, trim the seam allowance close to the stitchline.

5 Using the tip of the iron, turn the hem a second time to enclose the raw edges. Press as before to set the hem.

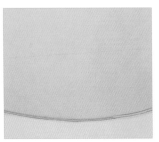

6 From the wrong side, machine stitch along the inner folded edge. Press again to set the stitches and to ensure the hem sits flat.

SHELL HEM

A shell hem creates a lovely finish to baby day gowns and petticoats. It looks especially beautiful when worked around the neckline and armholes of petticoats. It is worked from the wrong side of the fabric. Two blind stitches are worked between each shell.

Preparation Fold a 3mm (⅛") double hem. Press and tack.

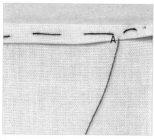

1 Secure the thread. Bring the needle through the fold at A, close to the folded edge.

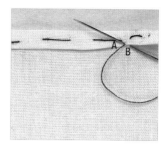

2 Pull the thread through. Picking up 2–3 threads in the fabric just below the fold, take the needle from B to A.

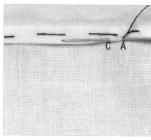

3 Pull the thread through. Slide the needle through the fold, emerging at C 3mm (⅛") from A.

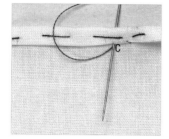

4 Loop the thread to the left and take the needle over the fold. Re-emerge at C. The thread is under the needle.

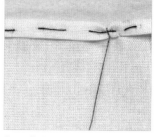

5 Pull the thread through firmly crimping the hem.

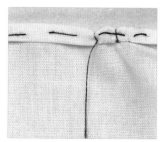

6 Work two blind stitches in the same manner as before. Repeat steps 4–6 to form the first shell.

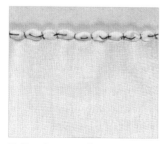

7 Continue working two blind stitches between each shell, spacing the shells approximately 6mm (¼") apart.

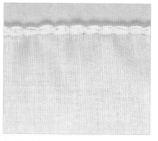

8 Right side of shell hem worked with matching thread.

Piping

Piping is a narrow fabric trim inserted into a seam to strengthen and define the edge.

CORDED PIPING

Piping is usually made by sewing a narrow cotton cord inside the fold of a fabric strip often cut on the bias. The size of the cord should be directly proportional to the weight of the fabric and size of the garment. For fine heirloom fabrics use the finest cotton cord and a bias fabric strip cut 2.5cm (1") wide.

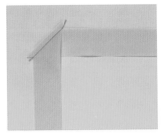

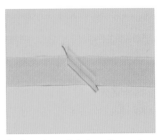

1 Joining bias strips
Place the ends at right angles and right sides together. Stitch diagonally along the straight grain. Trim the seam to 6mm (¼").

2 Continue joining the strips until you have the required length of bias. Press the seams open.

3 Making the piping Lay the cord along the centre of the bias strip on the wrong side.

4 Matching raw edges, fold the fabric over the cord. Stitch along the cord.

Hint

Use a machine presser foot that allows the cord to be contained within the groove underneath the foot. The most appropriate foot will vary from one machine to another.

5 Trim the raw edges so that the finished piping heading matches the width of the garment seam allowance.

6 Pull the cord equal to the width of the seam allowance from the end of the bias and trim.

7 Holding the piping with one hand gently tug the fabric to reposition the cord within the fabric casing.

ATTACHING PIPING TO A SEAM

When making the piping, move the needle to stitch one position away from the cord. Then, when sewing the piping into the project, use the needle position closest to the piping. This prevents the common problem of the first row of stitching being visible.

1 Matching raw edges, position the piping over the right side of the fabric and tack. Stitch along the piping stitchline, using a slightly longer stitch length.

2 With right sides together and matching raw edges, place the piped fabric over the remaining fabric piece, sandwiching the piping between. Tack the layers together.

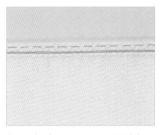

3 With the previous stitchline upper-most, stitch along the cording inside the previous stitchline.

4 Remove the tacking. Press to set the stitches and grade the seam allowance.

5 Open out the fabrics and press the seam allowance to one side.

ATTACHING PIPING TO A CORNER

Mark the corner point of the stitchline using a chalk pencil or water-soluble fabric marker.

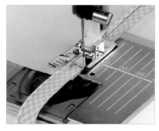

1 Stitch the piping to within 13mm (½") of the corner, stopping with the needle in the fabric.

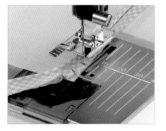

2 Lift the presser foot. Using small, sharp pointed scissors, clip the piping heading at the corner point and again 6mm (¼") on each side of the corner.

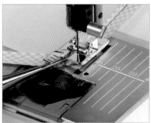

3 Shorten the stitch length, stitch to the corner point, pushing against the piping cord with a stiletto to add ease for the turn.

Hint

Many vintage garments included the tiniest cording or piping to add detail around the armhole and at the yoke or waistline. Baby and children's clothing can be brought to life with the addition of piped seams in contrasting fabric.

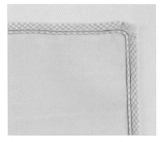

4 Stop with the needle in the fabric and lift the presser foot. Pivot and make one diagonal stitch across the corner, turning the flywheel by hand. Stop with the needle in the fabric.

5 Pivot again. Continue stitching along the adjacent side. Use the stiletto to push against the cord.

6 Increase to the regular stitch length and continue stitching.

ATTACHING PIPING TO A CURVED EDGE

For the best result when stitching piping on the small curves, use a manual buttonhole foot, decentre the needle and position the piping under one of the grooves on the foot.

Preparation Trim the piping heading to the same measurement as the garment piece.

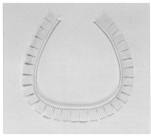
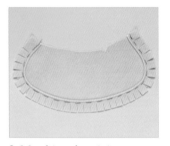
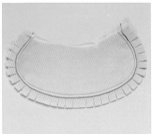

1 Cut a length of piping to fit the curved edge. Clip the piping heading at 6mm (¼") intervals or as required by the shape of the curve.

2 Matching the piping stitchline to the garment stitchline, pin and tack the piping to the right side of the fabric ensuring there is ample ease in the cord to the right side.

3 Stitch the piping in place along the piping stitchline. Remove the tacking.

Plackets

A placket is a functional detail, neatening a partial opening and allowing the wearer to get in and out of the garment with ease. A fitted garment, such as a dress with a fitted waistline, will require a longer placket than a loosely fitted garment such as an A-line dress.

Size	Garment with no Waistline (Bishop, A-line Dress or Daygown)	Garment with a Waistline (Placket in Skirt only)
6 months	19cm (7½")	10cm (4")
1	21cm (8¼")	10cm (4")
2	22cm (8⅝")	11.5cm (4½")
3	23cm (9")	11.5cm (4½")
4	24cm (9½")	12.5cm (5")
5	25.5cm (10")	12.5cm (5")
6	28cm (11")	13.5cm (5¼")
7	29.5cm (11⅝")	14cm (5½")
8	31cm (12¼")	15cm (6")

BABY PLACKET

This technique is used for openings in fabric without a seam and forms a small pleat at the base of the placket. It creates a delicate finish, particularly when worked by hand.

Preparation At the required position, rule a line at a right angle to the raw edge, slightly shorter than the finished length of the opening. Cut along the line.

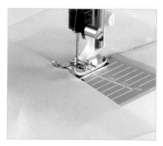

1 Stitching from the upper edge, roll and whip the edge, keeping the right hand side of the fabric out of the way.

2 At the base of the placket, work two or three stitches as you pivot the fabric, turning the fly wheel by hand.

Suggested machine settings

Zigzag stitch:
W: 2.0–2.5, L: 0.75–1.0
Presser foot: all purpose

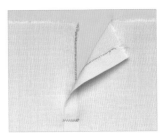

3 Roll and whip the remaining side of the opening.

4 Bring the neatened edges together. Forming a small pleat at the base of the placket, fold and press the overlap to the wrong side, leaving the underlap extended. Press.

5 **Optional** Hand or machine stitch across the base of the placket to hold the pleat in place.

CONTINUOUS LAPPED PLACKET

Unseamed fabric

This is the strongest and most suitable option for openings into fabric without a seam.

Preparation Mark a line slightly shorter than the finished length of the opening, at a right angle to the raw edge.

1 Staystitch along both sides of the marked line, beginning 3mm (⅛") away at the upper edge and tapering to a point at the lower end.

2 Cut along the line, taking care not to cut the stitching at the point. Spread the cut edges. With right sides together, position the staystitching just above the placket stitchline.

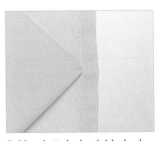

3 Pin, tack and stitch with the garment uppermost, taking care not to form a pleat at the centre.

4 Press under the seam allowance on the remaining long edge of the placket strip. Fold the placket over the seam allowance to the wrong side and tack in place.

5 Handstitch the folded edge to the previous stitchline.

6 Fold the placket with right sides together. Pin and stitch a diagonal line a the folded base of the placket.

7 Press the overlap of the placket to the wrong side and leave the underlap extended.

CONTINUOUS LAPPED PLACKET

French seam

A continuous lapped placket is a suitable option for openings into French seams.

Preparation Cut the placket piece twice the length of the placket opening and 4cm (1½") wide.

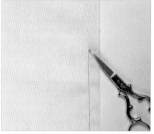

1 Stitch the first seam of the French seam to the placket point. Clip the seam allowance, angling the cut up towards the end of the placket opening.

2 Complete the French seam below the clipped point. Press the seam to one side.

3 With right sides together, pin and tack the placket piece along both sides of the opening, taking care not to form a pleat at the centre.

4 Stitch with the garment uppermost, ensuring the first stitch of the French seam is caught in the stitching.

5 Press the seam towards the placket. Press under the seam allowance on the remaining long side of the placket strip.

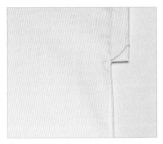

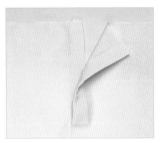

6 Fold the pressed edge over the seam allowance to the wrong side. Pin and tack. Handstitch along the previous stitchline.

7 Remove the tacking and press. Fold the placket with right sides together. Pin and stitch diagonally across the base of the placket.

8 Press the overlap of the placket to the wrong side and leave the underlap extended.

DOUBLE LACE PLACKET

This placket is most suitable for very lightweight fabrics. It works very well when used in conjunction with a French seam. It encloses the raw edges that are created when a French seam is stopped partway through its length in order to accommodate the placket.

Preparation Measure and mark the length of the placket opening.

1 Measure and cut three pieces of lace insertion, each 1.5cm (⅝") longer than the opening.

2 Starting at the base of the placket opening, join the two garment pieces with a French seam. Cut the seam allowance at the top of the seam to the stitchline.

3 Press the French seam to one side and press open the seam allowance along the placket opening.

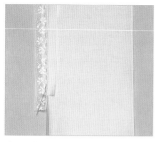 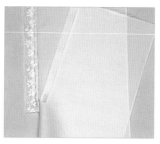 

4 With right sides together and matching the stitchline of the opening with the lace heading, tack one piece of lace to the placket opening with the excess extending past the opening.

5 Using a short straight stitch, stitch in place along the lace heading. Press to set the stitches.

6 Zigzag over the previous stitchline and remove the tacking.

7 Wrong side Trim the seam allowance close to the zigzag. Press the lace back behind the garment piece.

8 With wrong sides together and matching the lace pattern, stitch the remaining two pieces of lace together along one side with a narrow zigzag, enclosing the edges.

9 Open out the lace. With the right side facing, place one heading on the stitchline along the placket opening. Tack in place.

10 Straight stitch in place along the lace heading.

11 Remove the tacking and press the seam allowance back behind the garment.

12 Fold the lace placket in half along the join, aligning the heading with the stitchline and tack in place.

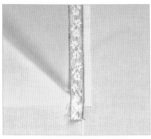

13 Folding the other side of the opening out of the way and starting at the upper edge, zigzag through both lace headings continuing through the allowance of the French seam.

14 To finish, sew across the base of the placket through all three lace pieces. Trim the whiskers and remaining seam allowance.

15 Completed placket.

EXTENSION PLACKET

This type of placket is perfect for an opening along a seam. The seam allowance into which the placket will be incorporated will need to measure at least 18mm (¾"). In the case of a smocked bishop dress, leave 2.5cm (1") unpleated at each end to form the foundation of the placket.

Preparation Cut a facing from the garment fabric on the straight grain 4.5–5cm (1¾"–2") wide and 18mm (¾") longer than the opening.

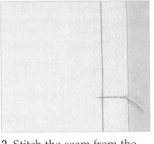

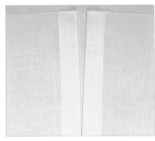

1 Neaten the seam edges along the length of the garment. Measure and tack the length of the placket.

2 Stitch the seam from the upper raw edge to the lower edge of the placket with a long basting stitch. Secure the stitches at this point. Continue stitching to the hemline with a short stitch length.

3 Press to set the stitches and press the seam open and flat along the full length of the garment. Remove the basting threads within the placket opening.

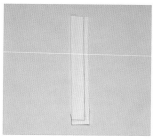

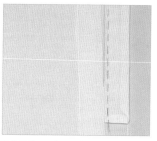

4 With right sides together, fold the facing in half along the length. Stitch along the length and across one end, using a 6mm (¼") seam allowance.

5 Turn to the right side, ensuring that the point is turned out sharply and press.

6 With right sides together and the seam open, place the placket over the single layer of the seam allowance, aligning the folded edge with the seam line. Pin and tack.

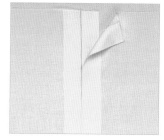

7 Using an edge-joining foot, stitch on the very edge of the placket fold using a short straight stitch with the needle off centre one position to the right.

8 Press to set the stitches. Using the side of the iron, press the seam allowance open. Only the placket facing should extend. The result is a neat, flat, invisible placket.

9 Wrong side Check that both seam allowances are turned back on the underside.

10 For a decorative heirloom placket, topstitch lace to the placket facing.

PLACKET CLOSURES

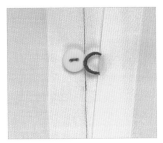

1 Snap fastener stitched to the placket extension and the underside of the overlap.

2 **Thread loop** Buttons attached close to the placket seam and button loop stitched to the fold of the overlap.

ROULEAU

Rouleau tubes make pretty trims when used with faggoting as a decorative feature, between two collars or for straps on a camisole or nightgown. Rouleau tubes are also useful as ties on baby jackets, bonnets and bootees.

Rouleau, or fabric tubing is made by stitching the raw edges of a narrow bias cut strip of fabric together and turning it to the right side. Rouleau is often made from the same fabric as a garment and used in place of purchased cord. When the fabric used is cut on the bias, the tubing is very pliable and can be moulded to follow the contours of a shape or to form loops.

Avoid using thick, bulky fabrics or those that fray easily or are difficult to turn. Always make samples from your garment fabric to be sure the tubes are correctly sized.

Preparation Cut a bias strip of fabric four times the width of the finished rouleau. Fold along the length with right sides together and matching raw edges.

1 Stitch along the centre using a very small zigzag stitch. When nearing the end, taper to form a funnel. Leave long thread tails on the funnel end.

2 Shorten the stitch width and length slightly. Stitch again just inside the first row, allowing the strip to stretch slightly as you sew.

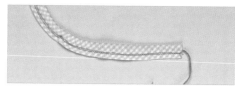

3 Trim the seam allowance so it is slightly less than the width of the finished tube.

4 Knot the long machine threads onto a tapestry needle or bodkin. Ease the needle through the tube and pull it out the other end.

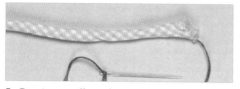

5 Continue pulling the strip through to the right side.

6 Press the rouleau with the seam along one edge or turned slightly to one side along the edge.

NARROW ROULEAU

Also shoe-string rouleau

Rouleau for ties, bows or loops will need to be narrower than those for faggoting.

1 Stitching 3mm (⅛") from the folded edge, stitch the rouleau following steps 2–4 for rouleau, stretching the fabric slightly as you sew.

2 After turning the tubing, wet it and squeeze it dry in a towel. Pin one end securely to the pressing board.

3 Straighten the tubing so the seam is not twisted and stretch it as much as possible.

4 Pin the other end securely and leave it to dry.

Seams

When stitching construction seams for heirloom sewing it is important to keep the seam as fine and delicate as possible. Reduce bulk wherever possible by grading and understitching. Avoid clipping into a seam allowance as it weakens the seam, unless it is the only option to achieve a neat result. Concave and convex curves with an inconspicuous seam allowance can be created by stitching with a short stitch length (not more than 1.8–2.0). Grade the seam allowance with the greater amount of the allowance to the outside of the garment, ensuring the finished seam allowance is no more than 4mm (³⁄₁₆"). Use your thumb rather than any sharp implement to gently smooth the curve.

DECORATIVE SEAM

A seam can be turned into a design feature without the need for neatening the seam allowances. This treatment works well for joining a yoke to a skirt, attaching a ruffle to the edge of a daygown or an eyelet edge to a sleeve.

A decorative ribbon, tape or Swiss beading is placed over the seam.

1 Construct a plain or gathered seam with the seam allowance on the right side of the garment. Press to set the stitches.

2 Trim or grade the seam allowances so they are less than the width of the trim. Press the seam in the direction it will lay once the trim has been added.

3 Centre the trim over the seam, covering the raw edges and stitchline. Tack in place.

4 Stitch the trim in place along the upper and lower edge. Remove any visible gathering threads.

FRENCH SEAM

French seams are particularly suited to sheer or lightweight fabrics. They form a beautiful finish on the inside of the garment, while fully enclosing the raw edges.

Preparation. Cut the seam allowances no lessthan 1cm (⅜") to accommodate the French seam.

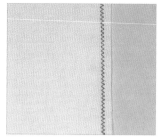

1 With wrong sides together, stitch with a small zigzag stitch, ensuring the left needle swing is almost on the seam width line. Press to set the zigzag stitches.

Suggested machine settings

Zigzag stitch
W: 2.0 L: 1.2 – 1.5
Foot: all-purpose
Needle position: centre to right
Straight stitch
L: 1.8 – 2.0
Foot: standard or ¼"
Needle position: centre

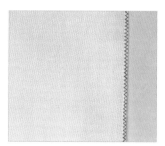

2 Trim the seam allowance very close to the zigzag, taking care not to cut the stitches.

3 With the zigzag seam facing, press the seam flat from both sides of the stitching, using the side of the iron to push firmly against the stitches.

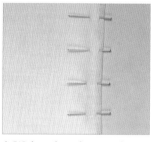

4 With right sides together, roll the seam between your fingers creating a sharp edge along the previous stitchline. Pin together and tack if necessary on a curved line.

Hint

1 Always stitch the first row (wrong sides together) and the second row (right sides together) in the same direction to avoid the seam twisting or wrinkling.

2 When working along a curved edge, tack the layers together.

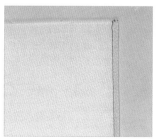

5 Straight stitch along the seam 3–5mm (⅛–³⁄₁₆") from the edge, enclosing the raw edges.

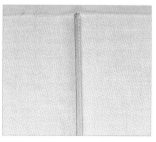

6 Press to set the stitches. Press the seam flat and to one side.

7 Press again from the right side.

GATHERED FRENCH SEAM

The gathered French seam is particularly useful when attaching puffed sleeves in lingerie or baby gown, ruffles to a skirt or joining the skirt to a bodice.

A finished French seam on sheer or lightweight fabrics should not exceed 5mm (³⁄₁₆") finished width.

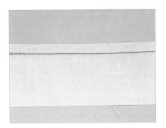

1 **Gathering** Stitch the first row of machine gathering just outside the stitchline

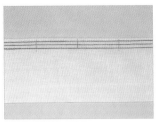

2 Stitch another two machine gathering rows evenly spaced within the seam allowance. Mark the half and quarter points on both pieces of fabric.

3 Gently pull the bobbin threads and gather the fabric to the correct measurement.

4 With wrong sides together, matching raw edges and the gathered fabric uppermost, stitch the pieces together between the second and third gathering rows, using a narrow zigzag.

5 Press to set the stitches. Trim away the excess seam allowance, trimming close to the zigzag.

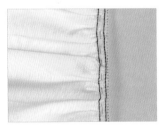

6 With right sides together, roll the seam between your fingers creating a sharp edge along the pervious stitchline and tack.

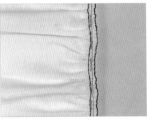

7 With the gathered fabric uppermost, straight stitch on the seam line, no more than 5mm (³⁄₁₆") from the folded edge, enclosing the zigzag stitches within the seam.

8 Remove the tacking and visible gathering stitches. Press to set the stitches and press the seam away from the gathered fabric. Sample stitched using matching thread.

SELF BOUND SEAM

The self bound seam is so named as one seam allowance wraps around and binds the other. The self bound seam looks similar to a French seam but is not as durable. It works best on lightweight fabrics that do not fray easily. On fine, single thickness fabrics, accurate results can be achieved with a 1cm (⅜") seam allowance, but you would be wise to consider using a 1.5cm (⅝") seam allowance where one layer of fabric has been gathered.

1 With right sides together and raw edges even, stitch the seam.

2 Trim one seam allowance to one-third the width of the other, 3mm (⅛") on a 1cm (⅜") seam.

3 Turn under one third of the wider, seam allowance and press. The raw edges should meet along the centre.

4 Turn the folded edge to lay along the stitchline, enclosing the raw edges and tack in place.

5 Topstitch close to the first stitchline

6 Remove the tacking and press to set the stitches. Press the seam over the second fold.

7 Alternatively, whipstitch the folded edge to the first stitchline.

Index

A

Adjusting machine settings, 25, 42
All-purpose foot, 5
Attaching curved lace to curved lace, 82
Attaching entredeux to entredeux, 27
Attaching entredeux to a concave curve, 32
Attaching entredeux to a convex curve, 32
Attaching entredeux to a corner, 33, 35
Attaching entredeux to a mitred lace corner, 38
Attaching entredeux to fabric by hand, 28
Attaching entredeux to fabric by machine, 29, 30
Attaching entredeux to flat lace, 36
Attaching entredeux to gathered fabric, 31
Attaching entredeux to gathered lace, 37
Attaching entredeux to puffing, 57
Attaching gathered lace to fabric, 76
Attaching lace to fabric, pin stitch, 73
Attaching lace to fabric, rolled seam, 70, 71, 72
Attaching lace to lace, 81
Attaching lace to ricrac, 92
Attaching lace to ruched ribbon edge, 112
Attaching lace to scalloped edge, 74

Attaching lace with faggoting, 103
Attaching piping to a corner, 125
Attaching piping to a curved edge, 126
Attaching piping to a seam, 125

B

Baby placket, 127
Baby ricrac edge, 91
Baby ricrac and lace edge, 92
Basic presser foot, 5
Basic tuck by machine, 61
Beads to buttonhole stitch edge, 97
Beaded ruched edging, 110
Beading, 17
Bias, 11
Bias and curves, 43
Blanket stitch and buttonhole stitch edges, 93–95, hints, 94, 95
Blanket stitch edge, 93, 95
Blanket stitch scallops, 98
Blocking board, 9
Boxes, 23
Braid, 14
Broderie anglaise, 16
Bullion scallop edge, 99
Buttonhole stitch edge, 94
Buttonhole stitch to entredeux, 96
Buttonhole stitch with beads, 97
Buttonholes, 113–117, hints, 114, 116
Buttons, 14

Button and buttonhole placement, 113, hint, 116
Buttonhole stitch to entredeux, 96

C

Chalk based pencil, 8, 19
Clear grid rule, 9
Construction techniques, 113–139
  Buttons and buttonholes 113–117
  Hems, 47, 51, 118–123
  Piping, 124–126
  Plackets, 127–134
  Rouleau, 134–135
  Seams, 136–139
Continuous lapped placket, 128, 129
Corded piping, 124
Corded edge, 45, hint, 46
Corded tuck, 62, 67, hint, 62
Cordonnet, 16
Crochet scallop edge, 100
Corded twin needle tuck, 67
Creating lace insertions, 83
Cross grain, 11
Curves, 32, 43, hint, 46
Cutting buttonholes, 114
Cutting out, 18

D

Decorative seam, 20, 120, 121, 136, hint, 85
Decorative thread replacement, 102
Detergent, 22
Ditch, 16
Double lace placket, 130
Drawing threads, 60, 102, 105

Dressmaking scissors, 7
Dressmaking square, 9
Drying, 22
Duck-bill scissors, 7

E

Edge-joining foot, 5
Edging, 16
Embroidery foot, 6
Embroidery scissors, 7
Encased thread gathering, 44
Entredeux, 16, 25, hints, 25, 29, 36
Entredeux techniques, 25–38
  Adjusting machine settings, 25 hint, 29
  Attaching entredeux to entredeux, 27
  Attaching entredeux to fabric, 28–35
  Attaching entredeux to lace, 36–38
  Buttonhole stitch to entredeux, 96
  Crochet scallop edge, 100
  Sewing entredeux, 25
  Joining entredeux, 26
  Puffing with entredeux, 57
  Trimming entredeux, 26, 27
Equipment, 5–9
Extension placket, 132

F

Fabric, 10–13, 18
Fabric marking pen, 8, 19, hint, 68
Fabric techniques, 39–69
  Corded edge, 45

Encased thread gathering, 44
Fine roll hem, 40
French roll hem, 39
Gathering, 44
Madeira Appliqué, 47–52
Mock roll hem, 39
Puffing, 53–57
Roll and whip, 40–44, hint, 41
Tucks, 59–69, hints, 59, 60, 62
Fading markers, 9, 19
Faggoting, 103
Fasteners, 14
Fine roll hem, 40
Finishing, 21
Flexible French curve, 9
Folded straight hem, 47
French rolled hem, 39
French seam, 129, 137, 138

G

Galloon, 16
Garment records, 23
Gathered French seam, 138
Gathering lace, 76
Gathering fabric, 20, 31, 44, 53, 55, 86 hint, 87
General instructions, 18–21
General tools, 9
Gimp thread, 16
Grain, 11
Grading, 20

H

Hanging, 22
Handloom, 16
Handworked buttonholes, 115

Handworked edges and finishes, 91–112
  Baby ricrac edges, 91, 92
  Blanket stitch and buttonhole stitch edges, 93–98, hints, 94, 95
  Bullion scallop edge, 99
  Crochet scallop edge, 100
  Decorative thread replacement, 102
  Faggoting, 103

Hemstitch, 104–107
Palestrina knot edge, 108
Ruched edges, 109–112
Heading, 16
Hem marker, 9
Hem tuck, 119
Hem tuck with Swiss edging, 120, 121
Hemming into tuck, 118
Hems, 47, 51, 118–123

Hemstitch, 104, 105 hints,
    85, 107
Holes in lace seams, 81
Hooks and eyes, 14

I

Interfacing, 13
Inserting lace into flat
    fabric, 84, 88
Inserting lace into gathered
    fabric, 86
Inserting lace into
    scallops, 88
Insertion lace, 16, 83, hint, 87
Insertion lace shapes, 89
Invisible lace join, 79
Iron, 8
Ironing, 22
Ironing board, 8

J

Jeans foot, 5
Joining entredeux, 26
Joining holes in lace
    seams, 81
Joining lace, 79
Joining new thread, 95

L

Lace, 16, 70–90
Lace edges by hand, 92,
    103, 112
Lace edges by machine,
    70–76
Lace fabric, 81
Lace, gathering, 76
Lace heading, 16, 76
Lace insertion, 16, 17, 83–90,
    hint, 87

Lace shaping board, 10
Lace techniques, 70 – 90
    Attaching lace to fabric,
        70–78
    Attaching lace to lace,
        81–84
    Gathering lace, 76
    Inserting lace, 84–90
    Insertion lace shapes, 89
    Joining holes in seams, 81
    Joining lace, 79
    Lace edges by hand, 92,
        103, 112
    Mitring lace, 77, 90
    Neatening lace ends, 80
    Shaping lace, 74, 82, 88
Ladder hemstitch, 107
Laundering, 22
Loop turner, 9

M

Machine maintenance, 5
Machine setting, 5, 25, hints,
    29, 42
Machine sewing threads, 14
Machine stitched
    buttonholes, 116
Madeira Appliqué, 47–52,
    hints, 49, 50, 52
Manual buttonhole foot, 5
Marking fabric, 19
Marking tools, 8
Marking tucks, 59–61
Marking stitch placement,
    hint, 94
Measuring gauge, 9
Measuring tools, 9
Medallion, 16, 56
Memory curve, 9

Mitring lace, 77
Mitring lace insertion, 90
Mock roll hem, 39

N

Narrow hem, 122
Narrow rouleau, 135
Neatening lace ends, 80
Needle position, 29
Needle threader, 10
Notions, 14
Novelty buttons, 114

O

Open-toe foot, 6

P

Palestrina knot edge, 108
Patchwork foot, 6
Pin and press tucks, 59
Pin stitch by hand, 48, hint,
    49
Pin stitch by machine, 50, 73
    hints, 50, 51, 85
Pins, 7
Pintuck, 61, 63
Pintuck foot, 6, 66
Piping, 65, 124–126
Placket closures, 134
Placket length chart, 127
Plackets, 127–133
Point de Paris stitch, 48
Pre-shrinking interfacing, 13
Preparing fabric and
    trims, 18
Presser feet, 5–6
Pressing, 21, 59, 69
Pressing tools, 8
Puff iron, 8

Puffing, 53–57
Puffing medallion, 56
Puffing using a sewing
    machine, 53
Puffing using a smocking
    pleater, 55
Puffing with entredeux, 57

Q

Quilting foot, 6

R

Release tucks, 63, 64
Repairing lace, 79
Reverse threaded release
    tuck, 64
Ribbon, 14
Ricrac, 14, 91, 92
Roll and whip bias and
    curves, 43
Roll and whip by hand, 40,
    hint 41
Roll and whip by machine,
    42
Roll and whip lace ends, 80
Roll, whip and gather, 44
Rouleau, 134
Ruche, 16, 109–112
Ruched fabric edge, 109,
    hint, 110
Ruched ribbon edge, 111,
    hint, 110
Ruched ribbon edge with
    lace, 112
Ruler, 9

S

Scallop radial rule, 9
Scallop template, 19

Scalloped appliqué hem, 51
Scalloped lace edge, 74
Scalloped lace insertion, 88
Scalloped piping, 65
Scalloped twin needle
    tuck, 68
Scissors, 7, hint, 46
Seams, 20, 136–139
Self bound seam, 139
Selvedge, 11
Sewing entredeux, 25
Sewing machine, 5, hint, 29
Sewing machine needles, 6,
    hint, 29
Shank button, 114
Shaping lace, 74, 82, 88
Shell hem, 123
Shell tucks, 65
Shoe-string rouleau, 135
Sleeve board, 8
Smocking pleater, 55
Snap fastener, 14, 134
Spray starch, 8, 19
Stabilising buttonholes,
    hint, 116
Standard presser foot, 5
Storage, 22
Staystitch, 20, hint, 52
Stem stitch on smocking, 58
Straightening fabric, 18
Straightening tucks, 69
Swiss edging, 16

T

Tape measure, 9
Templates, 19
Testing machine settings,
    25, 42
Thread loop, 117, 134
Thread tracing, 19

Thimble, 9
Tools, 7
Topstitch, 20
Trimming entredeux, 26, 27
Trims, 16, 18
Tucks, 59–69, 118–121,
    hints, 59, 62
Turned lace edge, 80
Turning peaks, hint, 52
Twin needle foot, 6
Twin needle tucks, 66–68
Twisted insertion stitch, 103

U

Understitching, 21
Universal foot, 5

W

Warp, 11
Washing, 22
Water-soluble marker, 8, 19,
    61, hint, 68
Weft, 11
Whipped tuck, 66

Y

Your finished project, 21

Z

Zigzag hemstitch, 107